Praise for *Wishful Drinking*

"What her Hollywood upbringing doesn't manifest intelligence and adroit way wit rare inhabitants of La-La land who can actually write."

—Charles McGrath, *The New York Times*

"Fisher makes each crushing tragedy hilarious."

—*People* (4 out of 4 stars)

"[Fisher] has a talent for lacerating insight that masquerades as carefree self-deprecation . . . The effect, ultimately, is extraordinarily painful while being extremely entertaining . . . [S]he's done her best to make sense of it all, and throughout, her humor has held up. In her own defiant manner, she's fought the good fight."

—Matthew DeBord, *Los Angeles Times*

"She's still funny as hell . . . Her stories bubble, bounce, and careen with an energy . . . Get someone to read this rollicking book aloud to you."

—*Entertainment Weekly*

"[T]here are also sparkling bons mots bespeaking [Carrie's] quirky intelligence and sweetness. Spoken like a true princess."

—*Elle*

"[N]othing, not even electroshock therapy to combat her bipolar disorder, has dulled Fisher's wit, which is as dry as the martini in the empty glass clutched in the hand of the passed-out Princess Leia pictured on the cover of *Wishful Drinking*."

—Richard Knight, Jr., *Chicago Tribune*

"Fisher is a language obsessive, a nimble verbal acrobat who puns and somersaults around a page with glee . . . If you are a fan of Fisher's fiction, a follower of her mental illness or simply a looky-loo stargazer curious about her Hollywood heritage, *Wishful Drinking* will likely make you laugh."

—Slate.com

"Clearly, you should buy this book. . . . she has expert comic timing and, perhaps more importantly, better stories than most drug addicts. . . . Fisher is unafraid to write, brutally and vividly."

—Maureen Callahan, *New York Post*

"Carrie Fisher can't stop writing or talking about her life, but who can really blame her? With stories like these, there's no need for her to hide behind fiction any more . . . Fisher writes movingly about what it's like to be born into celebrity and never really leave."

—*Variety*

"Fisher, unlike most celebrities (especially ones spawned from other celebrities) can actually write, and . . . *Wishful Drinking*, though an extremely short book, is super salacious and entertaining."

—Jezebel.com

"There are more juicy confessions and outrageously funny observations packed in these honest pages than most celebrity bios twice the length . . . With acerbic precisions and brash humor, she writes of struggling with and enjoying aspects of her alcoholism, drug addiction and mental breakdowns. Her razor-sharp observations about celebrity, addiction and sexuality demand to be read aloud to friends."

—*Publishers Weekly* (starred review)

"Engrossing and entertaining . . . Obviously, this is a one-of-a-kind life, and Fisher's story begs to be read aloud . . . a collection of caustically comical one-liners that prove Fisher's odds-defying resilience."

—*Wisconsin State Journal*

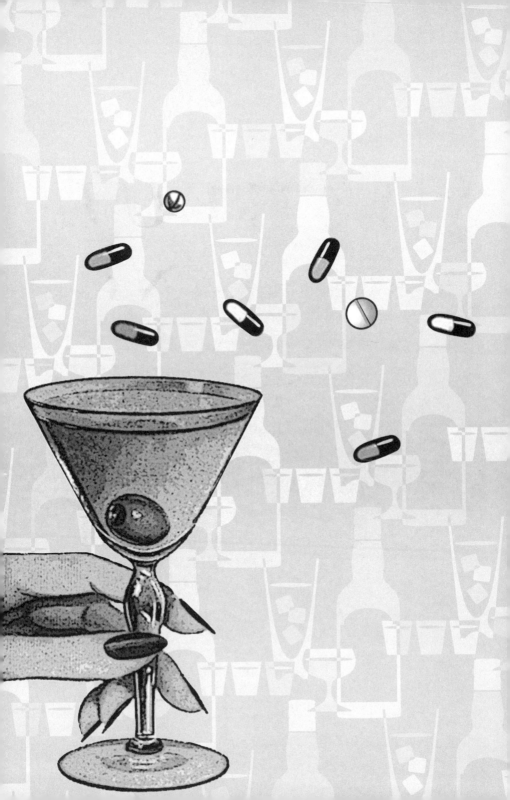

WISHFUL
DRINKING

CARRIE FISHER

SIMON & SCHUSTER PAPERBACKS
New York • London • Toronto • Sydney

SIMON & SCHUSTER PAPERBACKS

A Division of Simon & Schuster, Inc.

1230 Avenue of the Americas

New York, NY 10020

First Simon & Schuster trade paperback edition September 2009

The world premier of *Wishful Drinking* was presented at the Geffen Playhouse Los Angeles 2006.

Gil Cates	Randall Arney	Stephen Eich
Producing Director	Artistic Director	Managing Director

And subsequently at Berkeley Repertory Theatre

SIMON & SCHUSTER PAPERBACKS and colophon are registered trademarks of Simon & Schuster, Inc.

For information about special discounts for bulk purchases, please contact Simon & Schuster Special Sales at 1-866-506-1949 or business@simonandschuster.com.

The Simon & Schuster Speakers Bureau can bring authors to your live event. For more information or to book an event contact the Simon & Schuster Speakers Bureau at 1-866-248-3049 or visit our website at www.simonspeakers.com.

Designed by Dana Sloan

Manufactured in the United States of America

10 9 8 7 6 5 4 3 2 1

Library of Congress Cataloging-in-Publication Data is available.

ISBN 978-1-4391-0225-1

ISBN 978-1-4391-5371-0 (pbk)

ISBN 978-1-4391-5380-2 (ebook)

PHOTO CREDITS: © Bettman/Corbis: pages 2, 3, 4 (bottom), 5, 6, 26, 27, 29 (top), 31, 33–35, 38–39, 49; © Underwood & Underwood/Corbis: 3, 32; © Michael Ochs Archives/Corbis: 4 (top); © John Springer Collection/Corbis: 28, 29 (bottom); © St. Martin's Press: 67; Courtesy of Lucas Film Ltd.: 77, 78, 83, 84, 85, 89.

To my DNA jackpot—my daughter, Billie.

For all you are and all you will be.

I want to be like you when I grow up.

Happy days are here again . . .

So let's sing a song of cheer again

The New York Times

FRIDAY, MARCH 25, 2005

MYSTERY OF GAY OPERATIVE'S DEATH AT FISHER HOME

LOS ANGELES

ON the morning of Saturday, Feb. 26, a day before the Academy Awards, the actress Carrie Fisher woke up in her Beverly Hills home next to the lifeless body of a gay Republican political operative named R. Gregory Stevens.

Thus ended one of the more improbable friendships that Hollywood and Washington have known - and a globe-trotting, adventurous, but ultimately debilitating existence that might be fodder for a Tinseltown thriller, if it only had a satisf...

Before d...

the Middle East or the Balkans, depending on whom you believe, and he somehow acquired a mysterious piece of metal - this an autopsy confirmed - in the back of his skull.

"He thought "...rinsible." Ms.
F...
"The way he ...ving in a car

ens, in the ...s,
was ...wing life,
her about ...d maybe ...estate.

the Los ..., when coroner's conclusions, sounded comforted to learn that toxicology levels indicated Mr Stevens might not have been noticeably high when he arrived in Los Angeles. "I would've

Carrie Fisher often tried to help her friend with a drug problem.

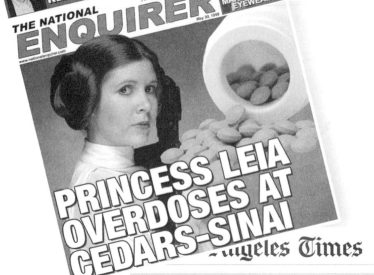

ACTOR ROBERT FORSTER FINDS NOAH'S ARK – READIES FOR FLOOD

ZELLWEGER HIDING IN MARC JACOBS EYEWEAR

America's Newspaper

THE NATIONAL **ENQUIRER**

www.nationalenquirer.com

May 30, 1999

PRINCESS LEIA OVERDOSES AT CEDARS-SINAI

...ngeles Times

CARRIE FISHER SAYS: "I'M BIPOLAR"

Hollywood star seeks treatment.

By LISA GREENE

Silver Hill Hospital is a nationally recognized, independent, not-for-profit psychiatric hospital. Since 1931, we have focused exclusively on providing patients the best possible treatment of psychiatric illnesses and addictive disorders, in the best possible environment - and it's still all we do because we both enjoyed dating and kissing. He was a darling person - I don't know what happened."

these programs provide treatment for the acute phase of a broad range of disorders, including schizophrenia and other psychotic disorders, mood disorders (including depression, and bipolar disorders), chemical dependency and alcohol abuse, eating disorders, dual disorders and personality disorders (such as borderline personality disorder because we both enjoyed dating and kissing He was a darling person - I don't know what happened." Soon after, romance inevitably blossomed in the fishbowl that is celebrity life, and the world fell in love with the young couple. Time Magazine wrote that they were "the entertainment

Patients with addictive disorders may be dependent on alcohol, cocaine, heroin and other opioids, tranquilizers and other substances. The treatment provided on this unit is a 12-Step oriented and is designed to provide medically managed detoxification in a safe environment. If indicated, this can include suboxone-assisted detoxification from opioids. Patients who enter the addictive disorders program are guided toward recovery and sobriety. Following detoxification, patients may be offered extended treatment in our 28-day Transitional Living Program, or may be discharged

Hi, I'm Carrie Fisher and I'm an alcoholic.

And this is a true story.

INTRODUCTION:
AN ABUNDANCE
OF APPARENTLYS

So I am fifty-two years old. (Apparently.) Actually, that's more verifiable than the rest of it. I'd better start off with certainties. Here are the headlines (head—in so many ways—being the operative word):

I am fifty-two years old.

I am Carrie Fisher.

I live in a really nice house in Los Angeles.

I have two dogs.

I have a daughter named Billie.

Carrie Fisher is apparently a celebrity of sorts. I mean, she was (is) the daughter of famous parents. One an icon, the other a consort to icons. Actually, that's not completely fair. My father is a singer named Eddie Fisher. What was, in the '50s, called a crooner. A crooner with many gold records. I only say my father is a consort because he's really better known for his (not so) private life than the life he lived onstage. His scandals outshone his celebrity. Or you might say that his scandals informed his celebrity in such a way as to make him infamous.

My mother, Debbie Reynolds, was in what might be called iconic films—most notably, *Singin' in the Rain*. But for whatever reason, when my parents hooked up it had an extraordinary impact on the masses who bought fan magazines. The media dubbed them "America's Sweethearts." The idea of them electrified—their pictures

graced the covers of all the tabloids of the day. They were adorable and as such were ogled by an army of eyes. So cute and cuddly and in some ways adorably average. The Brad Pitt and Jennifer Aniston of the late '50s, only slightly more so—because they actually managed to procreate—making two tiny children to fill out the picture. Or pictures, as the case turned out to be. An All-American and photogenic family.

When I was younger, starting at about four, other children would ask me what it was like to be a movie star's daughter.

3

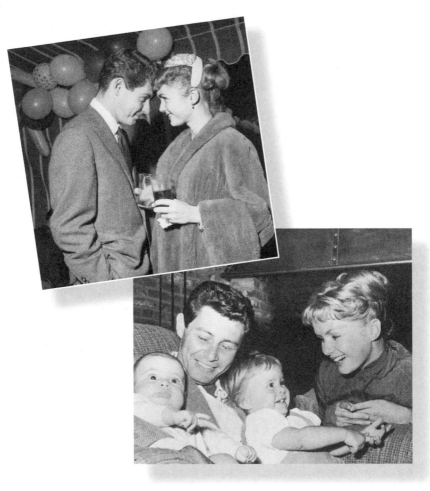

Once I was a little older and understood, to a certain extent, the nature of what celebrity meant, I would say, Compared to what? When I wasn't a movie star's daughter? When I lived with my normal, non-show business family, the Regulars (Patty and Lowell Regular of Scottsdale, Arizona)? All I've ever known is this sort of hot-house-plant existence, and I could tell from watching how normal people lived—normal people as depicted by Hollywood and burned into our consciousness—I understood that my life was unusual. Like many others, I grew up watching television shows like *My Three Sons* and *The Partridge Family* and *The Real McCoys*. And based on the lives depicted on those shows, I knew my life was a different sort of real. It was the only reality I knew, but compared to other folks—both on television and off—it eventually struck me as a little surreal, too. And eventually, too, I understood that my version of reality had a tendency to set me apart from others. And when you're young you want to fit in. (Hell, I still want to fit in with certain humans, but as you get older you get a little more discriminating.) Well, my parents were professionally committed to sticking out, so all too frequently I found myself sticking out right along with them.

Now, I'm certainly not asking anyone to feel bad for me or suggest that my existence could be described as a predicament of some kind. I'm simply describing the dynamic that was at work during my formative years.

My parents were focus pullers—and when I say

parents, I mean my mother, who raised me, and my father, who checked in from time to time.

I mean, if I came into a room and said, "You know how you saw your father more on TV than you did in real life?" I don't think many people would say, "Oh my God! You, too!"

And by the same token, I have to ask you, how often do you say, "in real life"?

Like real life is this other thing, and we're always trying to determine what's going on in this distant, inaccessible, incomprehensible place.

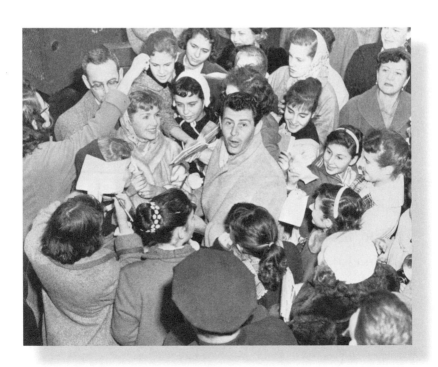

"What are they like in real life?"

"That happened in real life? *Really!*"

Stuff like that.

I am truly a product of Hollywood. You might say that I'm a product of Hollywood inbreeding. When two celebrities mate, something like me is the result.

I grew up visiting sets, playing on backlots, and watching movies being made. As a consequence, I find that I don't have what could be considered a conventional sense of reality. (Not that I've ever had much use for reality—having spent much of what I laughingly refer to as my adult life attempting to escape it with the assistance of a variety of drugs.)

So, as I said, my reality has been formed by Hollywood's version of reality. As a child, I thought that *Father Knows Best* was real and that my life was fake. When I think about it now, I may not have been far wrong.

I tell you all of this as a newly made bystander. As I have been reintroduced into my world by electroconvulsive therapy (more commonly known as ECT for those oh-so-fortunately familiar with it and electroshock for those who are not)—reintroduced to my life at the ripe old age of fifty-two. My memory—especially my visual memory—has been wrenched from me. All of a sudden, I find that I seem to have forgotten who I was before. So, I need to reacquaint myself with this sort of celebrity person I seem to be. Someone who was in an iconic, blockbuster film called *Star Wars*. (How trippy is that?)

One thing I *do* recall is that one day when I was a toddler, I sat planted closely to the television set watching my mother in a movie called *Susan Slept Here*. And, at a certain point there's a scene where my very young mother tilts her face up to receive a kiss from Dick Powell. A kiss on the mouth. A romantic kiss. So, she has her eyes closed, waiting. But instead of kissing her on the mouth, Mr. Powell bends down and kisses her on the forehead. I sit there, registering this and then look quickly over my shoulder to see if anyone else had seen what I saw. To see if I should be more embarrassed for my mother than I already was. I tell you this to illustrate that I didn't know the difference between movies and real life. In my life, they tended to overlap. Cary Grant (yes, *the* Cary Grant) became a family friend, even though he wasn't precisely that. And characters that my mother played in movies became confused with the person who was and is my mother. So in a way, movies became home movies. Home became another place on the movie star map.

Later on, I worked out that my mother's appearance

in the classic film *Singin' in the Rain* was not unlike my own appearance in *Star Wars*. When she made that film, she was nineteen and costarred with two men. I was also nineteen when I made *Star Wars* and appeared opposite two men. How this is relevant, I have no idea. Maybe I was just grasping around for a sense of continuity.

I emerge from my three-week-long ECT treatment to discover that I am not only this Princess Leia creature but also several-sized dolls, various T-shirts and posters, some cleansing items, and a bunch of other merchandise. It turns out I was even a kind of pin-up—a fantasy that geeky teenage boys across the globe jerked off to me with some frequency. How's that for a newborn-how-do-you-do damsel in very little cinematic distress?

To wit, one afternoon in Berkeley I found myself walking into a shop that sold rocks and gems.

"Oh my God, aren't you . . ." the salesman behind the counter exclaimed.

And before he could go any further, I modestly said, "Yes, I am."

"Oh my God! I thought about you every day from when I was twelve to when I was twenty-two."

And instead of asking what happened at twenty-two, I said, "Every day?"

He shrugged and said, "Well, four times a day."

Welcome to the land of too much information.

On top of all this celebrity parents and *Star Wars* stuff, apparently I was once married to a brilliant songwriter, a rock icon of sorts. I mean, this is a man who wrote an array of beautiful songs, and even a few songs that were about me. How incredible is that? And get this—I had always been a really big fan of his music. Huge. As a teen, it was just him and Joni Mitchell. And, as I couldn't marry Joni, I married him. I *loved* this man's lyrics. They were one of the reasons I fell in love with words.

How can you not love someone who writes "medicine is magical/and magical is art/ think of the boy in the bubble/and the baby with the baboon heart"? The answer for me was I couldn't. I couldn't not love him. I apprenticed myself to the best in him and bickered with the worst. And to top it off, we were the same size. I used to say to him, "Don't stand next to me at the party— people will think we're salt and pepper shakers."

And wait'll you hear this—I've written four novels. Seriously! And two of them were best sellers. My first novel, *Postcards from the Edge,* was adapted into a film directed by Mike Nichols, starring Shirley MacLaine and Meryl Streep, basically playing a sometimes better, sometimes worse, dolled-up version of my mother and myself.)

I could go on and on—because there are certainly a lot of other cool things. The coolest being that I'm the mother of this amazing daughter named Billie. She's my most extraordinary creation.

It occurs to me that I might sound as though I'm boasting. I promise you I'm not. It's just that ECT has forced me to rediscover what amounts to the sum total of my life. I find that a helluva lot of it fills me with a kind of giddy gratitude. Some of my memories will never return. They are lost—along with the crippling feeling of defeat and hopelessness. Not a tremendous price to pay when you think about it. Totally worth it!

But now that we've established that I've had ECT, I have a list that I thought I'd share. A list of the electroshock treatment gang who have also benefitted from ECT.

I do this because I find that I frequently feel better about myself when I discover that we're not alone, but that there are, in fact, a number of other people who ail as we do—that there are actually a number of "accomplished" individuals who find it necessary to seek treatment for some otherwise insurmountable inner unpleasantness.

I not only feel better about myself because these people are also fucked up (and I guess this gives us a sense of extended community), but I feel better because look how much these fellow fuckups managed to accomplish!

So here are a portion of the folks with whom I share electrocompany:

Judy Garland
Bill Styron
Sylvia Plath
Cole Porter
Lou Reed
Vivien Leigh
Yves St. Laurent
Connie Francis
Ernest Hemingway
Dick Cavett
Kitty Dukakis

I should also add that a lot of these people also show up in the alcohol addict line-up *and* bipolar crew (chapter nine), giving some of these multi-listers and myself the admirable distinction of having a trifecta score.

These fine folks are:

Bill Styron
Vivien Leigh
Frances Farmer
Sylvia Plath

Ernest Hemingway

Dick Cavett

Kitty Dukakis

Yves St. Laurent

Cole Porter

Why did I feel I needed ECT? Well, it had been recommended by several psychiatrists over the years, to treat my depression. But I couldn't bring myself to consider it as it seemed too barbaric. My only exposure to it was Jack Nicholson in *One Flew Over the Cuckoo's Nest,* which wasn't exactly an enticing example. From the seizures to the biting down on a stick to the convulsions, it looked traumatic, dangerous, and humiliating. I mean what do we know for certain about it? Aren't there a bunch of risks? What if something goes wrong and my brain blows up?

But I'd been feeling overwhelmed and pretty defeated. I didn't necessarily feel like *dying*—but I'd been feeling a lot like not being alive. The second reason I decided to get ECT is that I was depressed. Profoundly depressed. Part of this could be attributed to my mood disorder, which was, no doubt, probably the source of the emotional intensity. That's what can take simple sadness and turn it into sadness squared.

It's what revs up the motor of misery, guns the engine of an unpleasant experience, filling it with rocket fuel and blasting into a place in the stratosphere that is oh-so-near to something like a suicidal tendency—a place where the wish to continue living in this painful place is all but completely absent.

So, when weighing the choice between ECT or DOA, the decision is easy to make. Not only because of my daughter and the rest of my family and friends, but for my formerly high-functioning self. In the end the choice couldn't have been easier to make. Electricity as opposed to game over. I decided to ride the lightning instead of extinguishing the light of life that had once shone out of my eyes. I keep my wick lit for my daughter, Billie, for my mother, my brother—for my entire family—and for each friend I've made with both hands, one heart, two moods, and a head crammed with memory. Memory I must now reacquaint myself with.

Perhaps now is as good a time as any to share with you the message that currently greets all callers on my answering machine, crafted by my friend Garrett:

"Hello and welcome to Carrie's voice mail. Due to recent electroconvulsive therapy, please pay close attention to the following options. Leave your name, number, and a brief history as to how Carrie knows you, and she'll get back to you if this jogs what's left of her memory. Thank you for calling and have a great day."

Each night I do a show where I entertain with tales of my dysfunction. I've done the same show dozens of times in an assortment of cities, yet somehow—depending on the audience—it's always a little different. Adding myself to the dearth of damaged celebrities that seem compelled to share their tales of their time spent circling the drain.

Wishful Drinking—both the show and the book—chronicles my all too eventful and by necessity amusing, Leia-laden life. I tell this story, partly as a means to reclaim whatever I can of my former life. What hasn't been eaten by electroconvulsive therapy—and partly because I heard someone once say that we're only as sick as our secrets.

If that's true, then this book will go a long way to rendering me amazingly well.

1 SHORES OF EXPERIENCE BOTH DARK AND UNFRIENDLY

I have to start by telling you that my entire existence could be summed up in one phrase. And that is: If my life wasn't funny it would just be true, and that is unacceptable.

What that really means, other than what it sounds like, is, let's say something happens and from a certain slant maybe it's tragic, even a little bit shocking. Then time passes and you go to the funny slant, and now that very same thing can no longer do you any harm.

So what we're really talking about then is: location, location, location.

An example of the tragic and shocking might be: A few years ago a friend of mine died in my house, but not content to simply die in my house, he also died in my bed. So he didn't just die in his sleep, he died in mine.

Greg was one of my best friends. He wasn't my boyfriend or anything. Meaning he didn't die in the saddle, which would have made me the saddle.

No, Greg was gay. Which might turn out to be something of a theme in this book.

Now, if you entertain, like I do, try to alert your guests *not* to do this. For two reasons, really: a) They'll end up dead, and I don't care how religious you are, that can't be *that* big of a blast, and b) it tends to throw the hostess off her game. Like for a year or three.

Now I assume there might be some curiosity about this fairly exotic experience, and I realize we don't know each other that well yet, but I promise you that's going to change drastically until you might actually feel the need to divorce me, and for that reason there are lawyers standing by (but I promise you you're not getting a dime). Or maybe you're not curious about this because you've woken up next to a corpse and therefore already know a lot more than anyone could possibly ever want to about it. That or maybe you don't want to know what it's like. It sounds unsavory and distasteful enough without the details. So why dig deeper?

But actually, I've found that a lot of people are curious about this whole business of a man dying in my bed. One of my favorite questions an audience member asked was, "How did you dispose of the body?" As if I dug a hole, put Greg in a bag, dragged him outside, and . . . well, you get the overall gist of my drift.

Another favorite question is, "Were you naked?" I haven't been naked in fifteen years! I haven't even gone sleeveless in twenty!

Of course, sometimes people ask sensible questions, like, "What was he doing in your bed?" Then I get to say, "Not much." But when they phrase it the other way like, "Why was he in your bed?" I'm forced to reply honestly. I tell them that it was Oscar time in Los Angeles (which is sort of like New Year's Eve for the vapid). And as my home is one of the centers of vapidity on the West Coast, Greg had flown out to LA to accompany me to the parties. He'd flown in from Bosnia—where he'd been running a presidential campaign. Because that's what Greg did. He ran presidential campaigns in unstable countries—like Republicans like to do. So he and his assistant Judy flew in to stay with me. Judy slept in my guest house, and I had another female friend, who was gay, also staying with us. So I had a choice—sleep with the gay male friend or the gay female friend. I picked the gay male friend, and I was punished for it. I'll never do that again.

I've also been asked what the hell I was doing in bed with a Republican. And in order to demonstrate my loyalty to the Democratic party, I tell people that I may have *slept* with a Republican, but I've actually had sex with a Democratic senator.

Of course I'm then asked which senator, to which I reply, "Chris Dodd."

And the only reason I feel at liberty to blab about this indiscretion is that Senator Dodd spoke of our "courtship" that we engaged in those many thousands of years ago during his bid for the presidency some years back when Paul Simon (now a resident of Connecticut) helped him by supporting his campaign.

When asked to elaborate on our courtship, Senator Dodd coyly replied, "It was a long time ago, in a galaxy far, far away . . ."

I believe that it was largely this comment that was responsible for his failure to win the nomination.

You also might be wondering what caused Greg's death, so I'll tell you. He died from a combination of sleep apnea (you know where maybe you're a little overweight and sleeping on your back and snoring and you suddenly stop breathing; you know, it's kind of like you drown) and Oxycontin use. If you don't know what Oxycontin is—it's a *very* strong painkiller that has the nickname oxycoffin.

But Greg wasn't a Republican like a person who votes to the right. No, he was a Republican like I was Princess Leia. He was a Republican by profession. Because how many gay Republican drug users do *you* know? . . . Oh that's right, lots and lots. But Greg was really in on the ground floor of the whole gay Republican movement that's so prevalent in Washington today.

The fact of the matter is, Greg was a lot of fun—especially for a Republican, and he had great stories. I mean, this is a guy who had shared an office with Bush. But a long time ago. When Dubya was just George Sr.'s son. So they shared this little office and Greg once told me, "You know what Bush has as one of his many gifts? He can fart on command (in keeping with his jolly-college-good-old-frat-boy persona.)" And Greg said that what Bush used to do—when Greg would be expecting people for a meeting—W. would come in and fart in the office and then run, leaving Greg in the midst of it. Like someone in a cloud of marijuana smoke. And then the people Greg was meeting with would come in and, of course, they would find Greg surrounded by this awful smell.

It's not dissimilar to what President Bush has done to the country.

At the time of Greg's death, my friend Dave said to me, "Honey, I know this is a pain in the ass."

And I said, "If I could isolate the pain just to my ass, it would be awesome."

And Dave said, "Well, that's the meditation then."

You know what's funny about death? I mean other than absolutely nothing at all? You'd think we could remember finding out we weren't immortal. Sometimes I see children sobbing in airports and I think, "Aww. They've just been told."

But no, we somehow gradually just seem to be able to absorb the blow. Blow not being the operative word. Greg did do quite a bit of that—just not on this particular evening.

But enough about death, I just wanted to get that bummer story out of the way at the beginning of the book because all the rest of my stories are just fun and laughs and skipping!

2 SCANDAL OUTSHINING CELEBRITY

So now, will you come on a journey with me? We're going to start at death, but then we're going to double back and go all the way through an emergency room (where they know me), through Watergate, back through Vietnam to birth. My birth.

I was born on October 21, 1956. This makes me quite old—half a century and change. I was born in Burbank, California . . . to simple folk. People of the land. No, actually my father was a famous singer, and you wanna hear something really cool? My mother is a movie star.

She's an icon. A gay icon, but you take your iconic stature where you can. His name is Eddie Fisher, and her name is Debbie Reynolds. My parents had this incredibly vital relationship with an audience, like with muscle and blood. This was the main competition I had for my parents' attention, an audience. People like you. You know who you are.

My father had many big songs, but perhaps the one he's best remembered for was "Oh! My Papa," which I like to call "Oh! My Faux Pas." And my mother, well, she

did tons and tons of films, but I think the one she's best remembered for is the classic film *Singin' in the Rain*. But she was also nominated for an Oscar for best actress for her role in *The Unsinkable Molly Brown* but tragically, she lost to Julie Andrews, for her stunning, layered, and moving portrait of Mary Poppins. Ibsen's *Mary Poppins*, of course.

My mother was also in another film called *Tammy*, which was also a hit song—which pissed off my father because that was really his area. She was actually pregnant with me when she filmed *Tammy*. So if you look very carefully, there's a scene where she and Leslie Nielsen are in the garden trying to save some prize tomatoes in a rainstorm (like they do in old movies). Well, I am the bulge in the side of her abdomen. It's some of my best screen work; I urge you to see it. Oh, and she was also pregnant with me in yet another film called *A Bundle of Joy*, costarring the marvelous method actor—Eddie Fisher.

When I was born, my mother was given anesthesia because in those days they didn't have epidurals. (I always thought that they should make an epidural that works from the neck up, which was a condition I aspired to for most of what I laughingly refer to as my adult life.) Anyway, so my mother was unconscious. Now my mother is a beautiful woman—she's beautiful today in her 70's so at 24 she looked like a Christmas morning. So all the doctors were all buzzing around her pretty head, saying "Oh, look at Debbie Reynolds asleep—how pretty." And my father, upon seeing me start to come through—crown with all the placenta and everything else (ugh)—my father fainted dead away. So now all the nurses ran over to him, saying "Oh look, there's Eddie Fisher, the crooner, on the ground! Let's go look at him!" So when I arrived, I was virtually unattended! And I have been trying to make up for that fact ever since. Even this book is a pathetic bid for the attention I lacked as a newborn.

My father was best friends with a very charismatic producer named Mike Todd, who produced a movie called *Around the World in Eighty Days*, which won an Oscar for Best Picture.

So my father and mother and Mike Todd and his fiancée, who happened to be Elizabeth Taylor, went everywhere together—they went to nightclubs, on cruises—well, they literally traveled the world! So when Mike and Elizabeth got married, my father was Mike Todd's best man and my mother was Elizabeth's matron of honor! She even washed her hair on her wedding day. Now later I heard my mother mumble that she wished she washed it with Nair. But she's not a bitter woman.

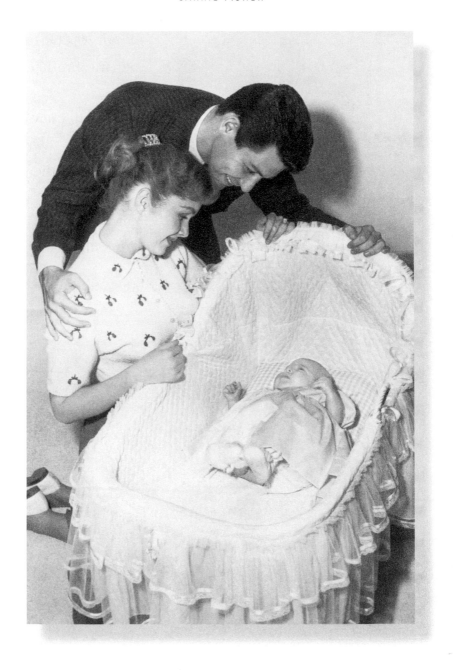

Anyway, I was about two when my brother was born, and my father so adored Mike Todd that my brother, Todd, was named for him.

Now, perhaps my father didn't realize that in the Jewish faith, it is considered bad luck to name a child after someone who is still living—a silly superstition—or so they thought!

Because about a year later, Mike Todd took off in a private plane in a rainstorm, and the following morning Elizabeth was a widow. Well, naturally, my father

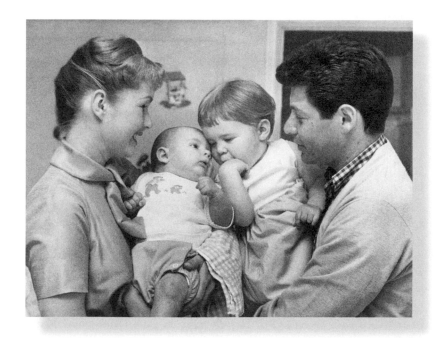

flew to Elizabeth's side, gradually making his way slowly to her front. He first dried her eyes with his handkerchief, then he consoled her with flowers, and he ultimately consoled her with his penis. Now this made marriage to my mother awkward, so he was gone within the week. And as far as I know he has not returned. Up to this very day. But you know what? I have high hopes because I think one night they are both going to come see my show on the same night, run into

each other, get that old feeling, get back together, and raise me right!

You might be thinking, well, that explains it! She's the product of Hollywood inbreeding. That's why my skull isn't entirely grown together at the back.

Recently, my daughter, Billie, who is sixteen now, had a flirtation with Mike Todd and Elizabeth's grandson Rhys. When they first met, they were trying to work out how it all fit together and if they were related in some way. So I thought about it. And when I think, I need an enormous chalkboard with a chart to hold my thoughts . . . because I have so many zooming this way and that and then it's helpful if I can have some pictures and a pen so I can organize the insanity that is my thought process.

Welcome, class, to Hollywood 101. Thank you so much for enrolling.

Photo identifications on page 163.

Alright, so up at the top left of the chart, we have Eddie and Debbie. In the '50s they were known as "America's Sweethearts." Now if you are too young to relate to any of this, try and think of it this way: think of Eddie as

Brad Pitt and Debbie as Jennifer Aniston and Elizabeth as Angelina Jolie. Does that help?

All right, so Eddie consoles Elizabeth with his penis, Elizabeth takes a movie in Rome—a big budget film called *Cleopatra* and she meets her costar Richard Burton, so goodbye, Eddie, hello, Richard.

These two hit it off like gangbusters (whatever that means) and they met and married and had a wild, passionate relationship with violet eyes and Welsh accents

and acting and diamonds and drinking, dancing and sex and joy and love. But ultimately, you know, with passionate relationships, they can become stormy, and then what do you think happens? That's right . . . they get divorced . . . but they have good memories of one another, so what do they do then? They remarry, that's right. Now, keep that in mind, because it might come up again.

All right, now let's go to Debbie. Now Debbie does not want to marry another man who will run off, so she marries someone very, very old who *can't* run—nope, Harry Karl can't run at all. All he does is sit in a chair and smoke and drink and read the paper, and after about thirteen years, he loses all his money, and then he takes all of hers. Fun! And so that marriage ends. And she was alone for a while, but then fate intervened and brought her this sociopath—Richard Hamlett. He has some money issues, too. Her money.

But let's not get too far past Harry Karl though. My first stepfather. Harry was a shoe tycoon. It doesn't sound like those words should fit together, does it? But in this case they do. So, prior to being married to my mother, Harry was married to Marie McDonald. Marie "the Body" McDonald. Now Marie was an actress(ish) and she and Harry met and they married and they had a wild, passionate relationship with bodies and shoes and drinking and dancing and lust and joy and fun. But here come the storm clouds. So what do you think they do then?

That's right, they do divorce.

But, they have good memories of each other, so now what do they do?

That's right, they do remarry and now they have that great American institution—they have make-up sex, which, as everyone knows, is the best sex of all, and they celebrate the great sex by having a child. And that goes so well that they adopt two more. But then the storm clouds come, so they . . . ?

Divorce.

Now, Marie MacDonald was a real romantic, an optimistic woman—and I say that because she married a grand total of *nine* times, which is a record for the board. And that's saying something, because this is a marrying board.

Now, that many marriages could give you a headache, no? Well, I think it gave Marie one because she became addicted to pain killers. Recently I learned this amazing thing. If you become addicted to pain killers, it can go very, very wrong for you. Who knew? Anyway, it did with Marie because she overdosed and passed away. And that last husband, not to be outdone, shot himself.

You might say they loved each other to death.

So now there are three children left. What should we do with them? I know! Let's send them to Harry and Debbie. Now, Debbie is told that one of the children should be institutionalized. But my mother is a good person, much like Sarah Palin (only smarter), and she says, "Absolutely not. We will put her in Carrie's room!"

(Sure, it's funny *now*.)

Now, Eddie. Poor Eddie. How is he going to follow an act like Elizabeth Taylor? Well, he manages somehow.

He meets a blond, cute, perky, fun, little actress. Sound familiar?

No, it's not Debbie again. It's a tribute to Debbie. It's Connie Stevens! They meet and have Joely Fisher, from sitcoms, and Tricia Fisher, from New York.

Oh, wait a minute—did Eddie forget to marry Connie?

He did! He forgot to marry her. But eventually they remember. So they get married. But as many people know, legal sex is just shite compared to that premarital stuff that so many couples have in cars, so they divorce. But don't worry, Eddie's not alone for long because now he meets and marries Miss Louisiana! She's three years older than me and she calls me "Dear," which I love. I love it! Now I thought this relationship would go on and on and on because Louisiana is in her early twenties and Eddie is in his late fifties, so she had so many years to devote to him. But what do you think happens?

Yup, they divorce. I was *stunned.* But don't worry he isn't alone for long. 'Cause now he meets and marries this really lovely woman named Betty Lin. She's from China and she takes excellent care of Eddie, and believe me, he needs it. And she's the same age as Eddie, which hasn't happened since the Debbie and Liz stuff. And the other good thing is Betty has a lot of money, which is handy because Eddie's gone bankrupt about four times by now. So they're happy together for ten or fifteen glorious years. But then what do you think happens?

That's actually a trick question because they don't divorce.

Betty passes away. But don't worry, he's not alone for long because now he dates all of Chinatown! He does this partly as a tribute to Betty and partly because my father has had so many face-lifts that he looks Asian himself. So that way they look like a matched set.

All right, so let's recap: Eddie and Debbie have me and my brother, Todd. I grow up, sort of, and I marry Paul Simon. Now Paul is a short, Jewish singer. Eddie Fisher is a short, Jewish singer. Short. Jewish. Singer.

Any questions?

My mother makes a blueprint, and I follow it to the letter. So Paul and I have a passionate relationship with a lot of words, big words, clever words, uh-oh, the words get mean so we get divorced. But don't worry, I'm not alone for long 'cause now I meet Bryan Lourd. Bryan is a talent agent, so fewer words, great sex. We celebrate and we have a child together. Billie Lourd.

Elizabeth and Mike Todd have Liza Todd.

Liza's a wonderful sculptress, and she meets and marries her art professor. Professor Hap Tivey. Hap is short for

Happy—so he's not Jewish. Anyway, they have Quinn and Rhys. So, Rhys Tivey and Billie Lourd—are they related? (You can peek back at the chart if you haven't already.)

I told them: "You're related by scandal."

I just hope the two of them get married so this will all be worthwhile.

And that is Hollywood inbreeding!

Hollywood inbreeding is sort of like royal inbreeding. And after all, celebrity is sort of like American royalty. So my brother and I are like those sad, sad cases like King Charles the Second of Spain. The last of the Habsburgs.

Charles was so horribly inbred that his aunt was also his grandmother. And his tongue was so large that he couldn't chew or be understood, and he drooled. Another little challenge was that his organs were dying inside his body (the one on the outside didn't work that well either because he died childless). But because his organs were dying, he actually smelled. So the people around him would put this perfume on him when he met prospective wives. (And by the way, we sell that perfume out in the lobby at my show.) Another issue for Charles was that he had these little seizures all the time and he would fall over, so the perfume people put weights in his shoes. Anyway, it worked because Charlie actually managed to marry twice, (probably someone with nursing ambitions), which just goes to show that there's a lid for every pot. Sometimes there are as many as nine lids for the same pot. Also when I was a teenager I could buy pot in lids. But I don't think you can anymore . . . can you?

Oh, and Charles's death caused the War of the Spanish Succession, which I know a lot of you have been discussing at length recently.

So my brother and I grew up smelling and drooling and having seizures, and we did all this in our house, which I called "the Embassy" because it looked less like a house than a place you would get your passport stamped.

Where would you put the Christmas wreath on something like that?

It was a modern house and it had things that most normal houses don't have. We had eight little pink refrigerators (you know, in case Snow White and the seven dwarfs came over) and we had a lanai and utility closets. Oh . . . and we had three pools . . . you know, in case two broke.

There was also my mother's closet—which I always thought of as The Church of Latter Day Debbie. There was a certain hush, a certain smell of Abolene cream and White Shoulders perfume. It was very quiet; it was very dark; it was subject to its own laws like the phone booth where Clark Kent was transformed into Super-

man. My mother's closet was the magical place that she entered as my mom and emerged as Debbie Reynolds.

Her closet was huge, like an enormous room, with an entrance *and* an exit, lined on each side by clothes of every sort—gowns, slacks, blouses, shoes and hat boxes, all manner of attire imaginable—and even the unimaginable. I remember she had these long pale gowns made out of beads. One in particular was a blue gown shimmering with blue beads. It even had blue fur on the sleeves and on the hem; she could float through a room in a movie star gown. Then, there was a long, shimmery, white chest of drawers where she kept all of her underwear and bras, and slips and stockings all neatly folded up and smelling of sachet. She had this weird, giant underwear that went over her belly button—big underpants and huge bras. I remember thinking, wow, some day when I'm grown up, maybe I'll get my own enormously big breasts. I used to watch while my mom lifted up her huge fun bags so she could wash underneath them. I eventually did get those big breasts, and now I'm sorry.

My mother's closet wasn't off limits, but it was very much hers and, therefore, my younger brother, Todd, and I valued it. It was prized because of how highly we prized our mother. She was often away, and when we missed her, we could go into her closet and do stuff like put our faces into a bunch of clothes and inhale the powdery, flowery scent of her. We would put on shows together in the closet, playing some kind of airplane game and restaurant game. And then there was this hat we for some reason called the "bum-bum" hat. It was this big straw hat with a brim that continued over your eyes with this green mesh you could see out of. We loved nothing more than to put on the bum-bum hat and look through the green mesh at our suddenly transformed surroundings.

My mother was magnificent when she was decked out in all her glory. When she was ablaze with all manner of jewelry and gems, shimmering diamond earrings and her neck encircled with bright stones that caught the light, a gown with matching shoes and stockings, makeup and her tall wig, carefully coiffed by her hairdresser Sidney Guileroff or "Uncle Sidney" as we were encouraged to call him. Sidney's name could be found in the credits of some of the more classic MGM films of all time. My mother would emerge from her dressing room a vision, so glamorous and so not of this world.

When my mother was at home on weekends, we stayed with her as much as possible, which frequently meant we were very involved in watching our mother. Right next to her closet there was this huge bathroom with magenta marble and mirrors everywhere. I remember the smells of her perfume—L'air du Temps—and of creams, like Ponds or Albolene. On the bathtub, there were always two or three monogrammed facecloths laid out—with her initials—DRK. Debbie Reynolds Karl. And then there was The Shrine of the Wigs, which was at the end of one countertop, along with what seemed to me like hundreds and hundreds of lipsticks and eyebrow pencils and false eyelashes. My mother was unbelievably meticulous at all of this. She'd twirl her hair up into pincurls that she'd use to pull her face tighter, then she'd put on her makeup base with a sponge. The base went low when the dress was low cut, which it usually was. Then she applied eye makeup and false lashes, so she didn't need mascara, but there was lots of eyeliner. Next came lipstick and rouge and powder— great puffs of glittering clouds of powder, followed by hair, which was a big deal, getting the wig on right. Then came the earrings, then she'd step into her clothes, and then came her stockings and her tiny little size five shoes. When she was completely finished, her Debbie Reynolds movie star accent got stronger, her posture got better, and she looked

incredibly beautiful. When our mother dressed, the man behind the curtain became the great and powerful Oz.

Undressing was also a process my brother and I observed. First we'd watch my mother as she removed her makeup with a wash cloth, then she'd take a bubble bath. As Todd and I looked on, Debbie Reynolds would slowly return to being our mother. The coach was once more a pumpkin, the footmen went back to being mice, Pinocchio became a real girl. We loved to be with her when she resumed her role as our mother. That this amazing being who looked like she looked and had these remarkable abilities belonged to us somehow. She was so beautiful, and of course I dreamed of one day looking like her. I fantasized that perhaps if Uncle Sidney would put my mother's tall, golden wig on my head and give me her perfectly coiffed hairstyle, then I would transform into the confident and shining beauty I would surely be. Soon I would be beautiful too. But to my horror, no such transformation occurred. It was then that I knew with the profound certainty of a ten year old that I would not be, and was in no way now, the beauty that my mother was. I was a clumsy-looking and intensely awkward, insecure girl. I decided then that I'd better develop something else—if I wasn't going to be pretty, maybe I could be funny or smart—someone past caring. So far past caring that you couldn't even see it with a telescope.

Sometimes my mother would take me shopping, to Saks Fifth Avenue, or a store called Pixie Town. But when I was a little girl (and even sometimes now), it was complicated to go out in public with my mother because she was very famous. She belonged to the world. She not only looked like Debbie Reynolds but to make matters worse she wore this giant big diamond ring. It was like being in a parade. In a way, my mother was an event. "Oh my god!" people would say to her. "I loved you in *Molly Brown!*" or "I saw you in Las Vegas!" So it was not like having private time with Mom. And I really didn't like sharing her. It seemed almost unsanitary.

When my mother was at home, she did a lot of sleeping, because she worked so hard and had such long hours, so Todd and I wanted as much of her company as we could get. So I slept on the rug on the floor next to her bed, and my brother slept on the couch near the window. In the morning when Todd and I got up, we would creep softly out of her room so we wouldn't wake her. Our house was very cold, with lots of marble and white couches that were all puffed up and glass coffee tables and white rugs with plastic on the corners to protect them. Everywhere were things that we could ruin, so we didn't want to screw up and make the puffed-up couch deflate or leave marks on the glass tabletops. It was complicated to find a groovy place to hang out in. We usually ended up hanging out in the kitchen. That's where it felt the homiest.

Now, my stepfather, Harry Karl, was not a handsome man but because he was wealthy and well-groomed he was said to be distinguished looking. That's ugly with money. They actually made a movie about Harry Karl and Marie McDonald and their multiple marriages called *The Marrying Man*, and Alec Baldwin played Harry Karl. I think the resemblance is astonishing.

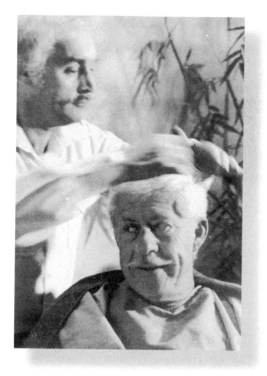

Harry had his own room with a closet that was pristine and beige. We had a laundress named Leetha who came in once a week just to do Harry's shirts. His shirts were monogrammed, and he also had monogrammed slippers and paisley pajama tops and a lot of neat gray suits. There was one of those black and red things that twirls around and shines your shoes, and a secret drawer to hide his gold coins and a wooden coatrack to put his jackets on.

He also had a man named Phil Kaplan who helped him dress. And then there was a barber and manicurists who came in to help him get distinguished looking.

But the most unique room we had was on the way to the projection room. It was like an exercise room, but what stopped it from being an exercise room was that it had a barber chair in the middle of it.

We found out later that the barber who came every day turned out to be a pimp with a talent for hair. And people who have pimps know that they can't do hair for shit. So those manicurists that the barber brought with him every day? They were probably doing more of a French manicure. The word "hangnail" comes to mind.

My mother, on the other hand, did everything herself. She was a very energetic human and could be unbelievably fun. Harry, though, was not fun. Not deliberately, anyway. But he did get out of bed wearing just pajama tops so the back of his penis was proudly displayed, and to top it off, he farted a lot, thus becoming a subject of great hilarity for my brother and me. We used to bring our friends over for a tour of the house, and if Harry was home, there were always gales of laughter.

Anyway, the whole manicurist thing made marriage to my mother awkward, so she took a musical in New York to get out of the marriage, which is a legal way to dissolve a union in Hollywood without involving lawyers. And so when I was about sixteen, my mother took

us out of high school, and moved my brother and me to New York for the year, and put me in the chorus of her show.

I don't care what you've heard—chorus work is far more valuable to a child than any education could ever be. I grew up knowing that I had the prettiest mother of anyone in my class, as long as I was in class. But even after, she was the funniest, the prettiest, the kindest, the most talented—I had the only tap dancing mother.

In New York, we all lived on a nice little street on the Upper West Side, sandwiched conveniently between a music school and a funeral home. Anyway, on one particular evening I was out on the town with some of the other "kids" from the chorus of the show, trying my best to be very grown up, as they were all at least ten years older than I was.

Well, somehow my mother knew what restaurant or club we were all at, so at about 10:00 or 10:30 someone comes and tells me that my mother is on the phone. Well, I'm not thrilled to have my hijinks interrupted by my mommy—reminding everyone I'm with that I'm far younger than they are and not to be taken seriously. Shit. So I grumble my way through the people and tables, making my way to the waiting phone.

"Yeah, Mom, hey—could I talk to you la—"

She interrupts me.

"I'm at the hospital with your brother. He shot himself in the leg with a blank."

"What???" I say.

"He'll be fine," she continues. "He's in surgery now—they're cleaning the gunpowder out of the wound. He's very lucky. A few inches up and—"

"He could've blown his penis off?"

"Dear—please—language. Anyway the police are here

and they want to come to the house to examine the gun. Apparently, if it can shoot blanks—oh, I don't know— they're saying it might be an unregistered firearm—or unlicensed—something, I don't know. Anyway . . . Where was I?"

"The police," I reminded her.

"Oh yes—now, dear, I need you and Pinky (my mother's hairdresser's name was—naturally—Pinky)— I need you to get to the house before the police to let them in, but also I need you to go through the house and hide all the guns and bullets and—what else . . . Oh yes! I need you to flush your brother's marijuana down the toilet. So you think you can do this, dear? Let me talk to Pinky."

Well, this part was kind of thrilling, I have to say. Who knew we had bullets and guns in the house? Granted, they were my stepfather's show guns that he wore ridiculously in some Christmas parade some years back, but it turned out it was considered a firearm! We were suddenly more like a mafia family than a show business one!

So Pinky and I rush back to our town house and hide the guns and bullets in the washing machine (they'll never look there!). And we sadly flush an enormous plastic bag filled with practically an entire lid of particularly pungent pot. Then I go out to check the scene of the crime—my mother's bedroom—where the shooting had occurred, and I have to say, it was quite something to behold. There are flecks of blood all over the walls and a considerable amount of blood on the bed. A sheet had been shredded in an effort to make a tourniquet. Wow, this was truly drama and it was happening in real life, of all places. My real life, surreal as it all too frequently became when I was living with my show business family and not the Regulars of Scottsdale.

But if I thought it was surreal at this point, it was about to get a whole lot surrealer. (I know—not an actual word.)

So now it's Saturday night in New York—you would normally think that this wouldn't be a particularly slow night for crime in New York—but you wouldn't know it by our living room, because we've got about five homicide policemen milling around, asking my mother pertinent questions about the crime like, "Did you know John Wayne? What kind of guy was he?"

Finally, they tell us that after examining the weapon in question that my brother used in commision of the crime of shooting himself in the leg with a blank, the five policemen establish that said gun could actually discharge live ammo and as such shoot actual bullets. What all this means is that my mother is in possession of an unlicensed firearm and needs to come down to the local precinct where she would be officially booked for possession of a firearm.

So now its about 4 A.M. and my mother and I are taken down to the police station for her mug shot and to be fingerprinted, along with the rest of the hookers, dope fiends, murderers, and thieves.

So by the time we get home it's close to six and my mother and I are at the kitchen table totally exhausted. Suddenly there's a knock at the door and we look at each other. Who could that possibly be at this hour? My mother gets up to see while I wait nervously. When she returns, she's laughing.

"What?" I ask. "Who was it?"

"It was a couple of reporters," she explains, catching her breath. "They heard Todd had been shot in the leg and they wanted to know if I had done it for publicity for the show. You know, to drum up additional ticket sales. I so badly wanted to tell them 'yes, and now I can only do one more Broadway musical because I only have one child left to shoot for publicity.'"

It's almost dawn and we're both so tired by now that we're a little punchy, so we begin to invent other reasons why my mother might have shot my brother. We came up with everything from he wouldn't clean his bedroom to he'd stopped feeding his turtle to his grades were down. (All perfectly credible, as far as we were concerned.)

The next day there's a photograph of my brother in the hospital with my mother in a mink hat smiling beside him on the front page of the *Daily News*. The headline read, "Picasso Dies."

Now, one detail I neglected to mention is that right after the gun discharged the blank into my brother's upper thigh, my mother was naturally frantic seeing all the blood on her only son. So she did what any mother frantic with worry for her child's welfare might do—she called a cab.

Anyway, cut to thirty years later. My brother arrives at Kennedy Airport in New York on business and he gets in a taxi to take him into the city. And as they drive along, the cab driver keeps looking in the rearview mirror at my brother.

Finally my brother asks, "Is something wrong?"

And the cab driver says, "Are you Todd Fisher?" and after my brother verifies that he is, the cabbie pulls an old, crumpled, bloody strip of sheet out from the visor over the front passenger side of the car and brandishes it for my brother to see.

"I drove the cab that took you to the hospital that night with your mom back in the '70s."

Of course he did.

So the cabbie has my brother sign the rag, brown and stiff with age, and then he drives back out of my brother's life—presumably forever.

3 A NEARBY ARRANGED ALL AROUND HER

My mother has moved into a house she bought next door from mine. There's this funny thing she does now, which is to offer my brother and me things that we can have after she's dead. If my eyes happen to rest on anything in her home, she rushes over and says, "Do you like this? Because I can put a little sticker with your name on it to mark it now. Otherwise I'll leave it for your brother." Of all her things, I guess I would want the blue dress with the blue beads and the blue fur. The thing is, I'm pretty sure it disappeared. But I still want it sort of passionately. I'll have to ask her to see if she can find it and if she does, ask her to put a red dot on it.

As a kid, I remember thinking, there is no other mother that even comes close to my mom. Then I became a teenager and thought she was an asshole because let's face it—it's a teenager's job to find her parent annoying and ridiculous—just ask my daughter. Anyway, after I was finished thinking she was this trippy lunatic, I realized that she was pretty fucking amazing. I mean, she's loyal, she's reliable, she's just totally great. Seriously. She's also really quick, and she can be really, really witty. She also still performs at the age of seventy-six, and she never misses a show—whether she's tired or her foot hurts; when she's out there onstage, she's radiant. This woman is the consummate performer. I've watched her for my whole life, and she's got this insanely strong life force. It pours through her veins and her muscles, and her heart. She's remarkable.

But here's the thing—she's also a little eccentric.

She's always had a lot of unique ideas. For example: She thought it would be a good idea for me to have a child with her last husband because it would have nice eyes! I should probably explain that my mother could no longer have children after having gone through "the Change," and Richard didn't have any children of his own and he had nice eyes!

Plus, my womb was free, and we're family. Now, my mother didn't bring this up just once or twice like a normal mother would. She brought it up many times—and mostly while I was driving. And when I finally suggested to her that this might be an odd idea, she said, "Oh, darling, have you read the *Enquirer* lately? We live in a very strange world."

Well, when the *Enquirer* becomes your standard for living, you're in a lot of trouble!

When I told my grandmother about my mother's idea, she said, "Well, that's not right." The voice of reason.

My grandmother Maxine is from El Paso, Texas. My mother's entire clan is from Texas. And my father's clan is from South Philly. So we're basically white trash. But because of the celebrity factor, I think of us as blue-blooded white trash.

I bring my grandmother up because when my mother was about seven my grandmother locked her in the closet. You know, for not finishing her dinner or her homework. (My grandmother was the one who told this story, by the way.) Anyway, after my mother had been in the closet for about an hour, she asked my grandmother for a glass of water and my grandmother, naturally, said, "Why?" And my mother said, "Because I've just spit on all of your dresses and now I've run out of spit and I want to spit all over your shoes!"

These are the people I hail from.

When I asked my grandmother later why she thought this form of discipline was appropriate, she said, "Well, we did not have *Cosmopolitan* magazine in those days so we did not know it was wrong."

Don't you think that my family has a really weird relationship with magazines?

Anyway, my mother and I never did go forward with the plan for me to have the baby with Richard, and I think that has turned out to be a good thing. Aside from the obvious—my sister, my daughter, my sister, my daughter—my mother ended up hating Richard and for good reason. He took all the money she had made since Harry took the first batch!

So she says to me at this point, "You know, dear, Eddie's starting to look like the good husband."

Eddie, The Good Husband by Anton Chekhov.

What could you say about my father?

My father is beyond likeable. I mean you would just love him. My father also smokes four joints a day. Not for medical reasons. So I call him Puff Daddy. But he is just adorable. There's a reason he got all that high-quality pussy—except for the Miss Louisiana thing, but anyone can make one mistake. So, after he wrote his— well, he called it an autobiography, but I thought of it more as a novel. After he wrote his novel, *Been There,*

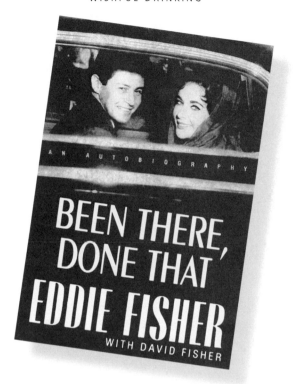

Done That—or as I like to call it, *Been There, Done Them* because it really was just about the women he'd ever slept with and how the sex was and what their bodies were like (so it is a feel-good read!).

But after I read it . . . well, for one thing, I wanted to get my DNA fumigated.

But I read it partly out of loyalty and partly because the *Enquirer* called to ask how I felt about my father alluding to the "fact" that my mother was a lesbian in the book. And not that it matters, but *my mother is not a lesbian*! She's just a really, really, bad heterosexual.

4
BOTH HANDS, ONE HEART, TWO MOODS, AND A HEAD

A few years ago my daughter and I visited my father in San Francisco, where he lives because there's a really big Chinatown there. And the day before, he had just gotten those tiny hearing aids that fit right inside his ears. They're really, really expensive. Some people say $3,000—others say five—anyway, really expensive. So he'd gotten them the day before, so the night before, he didn't want to lose them or forget where they were, so he put them in his pill box next to his bed so he'd remember where they were in the morning.

Yes, that's right, he ate them.

So, whenever he couldn't hear my daughter or myself, we'd yell into his stomach or his ass. Now he subsequently got those hearing aids again, and I had the opportunity to see them. They were the size of a lima bean—a rubber lima bean with an antenna.

Now look, I adore pills, I'm a huge fan, but these looked like none I've ever seen. Now, I don't know how you are in the morning, I'm not that sharp, but I think I would know if I was eating a rubber lima bean with an antenna! Twice!

Well, if you have a life like mine, then these experiences gradually accumulate until you become known as *"a survivor."* This is a term that I loathe. But, the thing is that when you are a survivor, which fine, I reluctantly agree that I am—and who over 40 isn't?—when you are a survivor, in order to be a *really* good one, you have to keep getting in trouble to show off your gift.

My mother says, "Well, dear, what are the choices? Not surviving?"

But this is from a woman who when asked for dating advice says, "For what age?"

My mother, who incidentally lives next door to me, she calls me to this day and says, "Hello, dear, this is your mother, Debbie." (As opposed to my mother Vladimir or Jean-Jacques.)

I have a very loud voice. I used to say that my voice was designed to wrest people from dreams. My mother grew up in Texas, on the border of Mexico, but she learned to speak "properly" with the assistance of Lillian Sydney, her vocal coach at MGM. Over time, she was able to gradually but completely lose her accent—unless she got really angry or frustrated with Todd and me—then she's been known to say, "Carrie Frances—y'all get your butts in here!" But my mom has what I can only describe as a movie star accent. It's very breathless and elegant—kind of mid-Atlantic. My brother and I frequently talk this way to each other now: "Hello, dear, this is your brother, Todd."

A few years back I interviewed my mother for this tragic cable talk show I was doing. This was for the Mother's Day show.

Anyway, we're chatting along pretty gaily for straight people, and then suddenly somewhere in the middle of our little chat my mother casually says, "You know, dear, it's like that time when I was a little girl and I was kidnapped."

Huh?

"Oh, darling, I told you about all of this, you've just forgotten."

(This was before my ECT, so there's no way I'd forget something like that. I doubt that even electroconvulsive therapy could banish a story as creepy as that one.)

So on she goes with this horrendous story, which I'm sure you're all dying to hear, like I was. Just desperate to hear each and every horrifically vivid detail of a tale increasingly tinged with darker hues of molestation. Happy Mother's Day everyone! After my panic subsides somewhat, I hear her saying that when she was eight or maybe younger, her eighteen-year-old neighbor and his friend scooped her up for a little joy ride. I'll spare you the more grisly details, but the good news is that despite the fact that something extremely unsavory occurred, my mother wasn't, in fact, raped.

Anyway, long gross story short, the father of the boy who encouraged my mom to consider a part of his anatomy as a lollipop called my grandmother and pleaded with her not to go to the police.

"I guarantee you I'll make absolutely sure he'll never do this again."

"How?" asked my grandmother, to which the boy's father somehow conveyed his intention to castrate his son.

"I'll fix him so he can't."

At this point my grandmother generously reminded the boy's father that he hadn't raped her daughter, to which the father allegedly replied, "I just wanna make sure he don't have the chance to do what he done again and maybe next time it'd be worse. He's disgraced our family enough."

Ah, the lovely family stories one has.

When I was about fifteen, my mother had started dating a man named Bob Fallon, and my brother and I called him Bob Phallus, because he came equipped with exotic creams and sex toys. You know, aphrodisiacs. Well, actually, Anglo-disiacs, because we're white. Anyway, thanks to Bob, that Christmas my mother bought both my grandmother and myself vibrators! As unusual as a gift like this sounds, you have to admit that they are the ideal stocking stuffers. I mean, you can fit the vibrator into the long top part of the stocking and still be able to get another cute little gift in the toe!

Well, I have to admit, I enjoyed mine, but my grandmother refused to use hers. She was concerned that it would short-circuit her pacemaker. She said that she had gone this long without an orgasm; she might as well go the whole way. (And that pacemaker, by the way, was later recalled.)

Now, look, I know you might be thinking that a lot of the stories I'm telling you are way over the top, and I would totally have to agree—but you can't imagine what I'm leaving out!

Anyway, I'd been singing in my mother's nightclub act since I was thirteen (like most teenagers) and I continued to perform with her until I was seventeen. The last show we did together was at the London Palladium, and I got pretty good reviews. So this choreographer contacts me and asks if I want to do my own nightclub act. And I thought, well maybe. I mean, I could end up being financially independent . . . and Liza Minelli—but you take the good with the bad. Anyway my mother thought this was a lousy idea. She thought it would be better if I

went to drama college in England because it would bring respectability to the family. Like we were a bunch of hookers, and drama college in England is the only way to eradicate a taint like that.

So now it's 1973 and I'm seventeen and I'm enrolled at the Central School of Speech and Drama in London. And, like I said, I really didn't want to go, but once I got there, it turned out to be some of the best times of my life. Truly. I mean it was the only unexamined time of my life, where I was just a student among students, going to voice and movement classes and learning weird little tongue twisters like:

All I want is a proper cup of coffee,
Made in a proper copper coffee pot.
You can believe it or not,
But I want a cup of coffee
In a proper coffee pot.

Tin coffee pots
And iron coffee pots,
They're no use to me.
If I can't have a proper cup of coffee
In a proper copper coffee pot,
I'll have a cup of tea.

Now if you enjoyed my performance as Princess Leia—and who could resist my stunning, layered, and moving portrait not-unlike-Mary Poppins performance—then it's thanks to tongue twisters like that.

Consider: "You'll never get that bucket of bolts past that blockade." Proper coffee pot?

Or: "Why, you stuck up, half-witted, scruffy-looking nerf herder!"—proper copper coffee pot, I'll have a cup of tea!

And don't forget, I had that weird little English accent that came and went like weather or bloat all through the movie.

And all my friends made fun of me because they said the title of the film sounded like a fight between my original parents—*Star Wars*!

5
ACCUMULATIONS OF INCARNATIONS

Forty-three years ago, George Lucas ruined my life. And I mean that in the nicest possible way. And now, seventy-two years later, people are still asking me if I knew *Star Wars* was going to be that big of a hit.

Yes, of course I knew. We *all* knew. The only one who didn't know was George Lucas. We kept it from him, because we wanted to see what his face looked like when it changed expression—and he fooled us even then. He got Industrial Light and Magic to change his facial expression for him and THX sound to make the noise of a face-changing expression.

Not only was he virtually expressionless in those days, but he also hardly talked at all. His only two directions to the three of us in the first film were "faster" and "more intense."

Remember the trash compactor scene in the first *Star Wars*? When Harrison and Mark and Chewie have just rescued me from my prison cell on the Death Star and we've just slid down the garbage chute and landed on a bunch of Death Star garbage and water? Well, under the water lived this serpent-like creature that in the script was called a Dianoga (though I don't think anyone ever referred to this thing by name in the actual film). So this creature, Dianoga, was meant to slither over to Mark, wrap itself around his neck, and strangle him as it pulled him under the surface of the water, leaving the rest of us up above to flip out. Well, in between takes of Mark simulating the strangulation, he would pick up a little piece of rubber trash and start singing (to the tune of "Chattanooga Choo-Choo"), "Pardon me, George, could this be Dianoga poo-poo?" (Okay, I guess you had to be there.)

Anyway, during one of the takes, Mark was so intent on making his strangulation look realistic that he ended up bursting a blood vessel in his eye, which in turn left this bright red dot. So, the following day we shot our next scene—which happened to be the last scene in the movie. You know, the one where I give out all the medals? Mark had to grin like a motherfucker in that scene in order to conceal his red dot. Because, ultimately, who's going to give a medal to someone with a big, stupid red dot in their eye? I don't care how much force is with him.

George also made me take shooting lessons because in the first film I would grimace horribly at the deafening sound of the blanks from the blasters and the squibs that the special effects team would place all over the set and on the stormtroopers. So George wanted to make me look like I'd been shooting them for my entire Alderaan existence. So, he sent me to the same man who'd taught Robert DeNiro to shoot weapons in *Taxi Driver* and so the shooting range was in this cellar in midtown Manhattan, populated with policemen and all manner of firearm aficionados. I used to have this fantasy that in some distant *Star Wars* sequel, we'd finally stop all the shooting and screaming at each other and would go to a shopping-and-beauty planet, where the stormtroopers would have to get facials, and Chewbacca would have to get pedicures and bikini and eyebrow waxes. I felt at some point that I should get—okay, fine, maybe not equal time—but just a few scenes where we all did a lot of girly things. Imagine the shopping we might have done on Tatooine! Or a little Death Star souvenir shop where you could get T-shirts that said "My parents got the force and jumped to light speed and all I got was this lousy t-shirt!" or "My boyfriend blew Jabba the Hutt and all I got" . . . etc., etc. You get the gist of my drift. But I have to admit, after a series of weapon instruction from a very pleasant ex-cop, I became quite proficient with an assortment of guns, including a double-barreled shotgun. Obviously my family was so proud. Because for fuck (or Darth) sake, I was always doing their endless stupid fucking boy things.

But back to the first film. Shortly after I arrived, George gave me this unbelievably idiotic hairstyle, and I'm brought before him like some sacrificial asshole and he says in his little voice, "Well, what do you think of it?" And I say—because I'm terrified I'm going to be fired for being too fat—I say, *"I love it."* Yeah, and the check's in the mail and one size fits all and I'll only put it in a little bit!

Because, see, there was this horrible fat thing going on! When I got this great job to end all jobs, which truly I never thought I would get because there were all these other beautiful girls who were up for the part—there was Amy Irving and Jodie Foster; this girl Teri Nunn almost got the part . . . Oh! and Christopher Walken almost got cast as Han Solo. (Wouldn't that have been *fantastic?*) Anyway, when I got this job they told me I had to lose ten pounds. Well, I weighed about 105 at the time, but to

be fair, I carried about fifty of those pounds in my face! So you know what a good idea would be? Give me a hairstyle that further widens my already wide face!

So you see, George Lucas is a sadist. But like any abused child, wearing a metal bikini, chained to a giant slug about to die, I keep coming back for more. Now why, you might ask? Well, (I would answer), let's face it, George Lucas is a visionary, right? The man has transported audiences the world over and has provided Mark and Harrison and myself with enough fan mail and even a small merry band of stalkers, keeping us entertained for the rest of our unnatural lives—not to mention identities that will follow us to our respective graves like a vague, exotic smell.

Speaking of graves, I tell my younger friends that one day they'll be at a bar playing pool and they'll look up at the television set and there will be a picture of Princess Leia with two dates underneath, and they'll say "awww—she said that would happen." And then they'll go back to playing pool.

And don't forget, George Lucas was the man who made me into a little doll! And it barely even hurt. A little doll that one of my exes could stick pins into whenever he was annoyed with me. (I found it in the drawer.) He also made me into a shampoo bottle where people could twist off my head and pour liquid out of my neck. Paging Dr. Freud!

And then there was a soap that read, "Lather up with Leia and you'll feel like a Princess yourself." (*Boys!*) Oh! And the nice people at Burger King made me into a watch. And you know Mr. Potato Head? Well, they just came out with a Mr. Potato Head Star Wars series so you might recognize me as Princess Tater? (With my husband Dick and our daughter, Rehabili-tater.) And I'm a tiny little stumpy Lego thing—which are delicious, by the way. And now there's even a stamp, which is totally cool—and not only because of the licking. But the thing I've been made into that has really enhanced the quality of my life? I'm a PEZ dispenser. True story. Which not only has really made my life great, but it's enhanced the lives of everyone I run into. If you can get someone to make you into a PEZ dispenser, do it. And my daughter loves it because like I told you, she's a teenager, and they love to humiliate the parent for sport, so all she has to do is flip my head back and pull a wafer out of my neck. But ultimately, I really don't mind. Even though, among George's many possessions, he owns my *likeness,* so that every time I look in the mirror I have to send him a couple of bucks! That's partly why he's so rich! Because I'm vain. So, I look in the mirror a lot, and it adds up.

You know I saw yet another Leia figurine recently at one of those comic book conventions—which yes, I go to when I'm lonely. Anyway, this doll was on a turnstile. And when it got to a particular place on the turnstile, you could see up my dress, to my anatomically correct—though shaved—galaxy snatch. Well, as you can imagine, because this probably happens to you all the time, I was a bit taken aback by this, so I called George and I said, "You know what, man? Owning my likeness does not include owning my lagoon of mystery."

Oh, and remember that white dress I wore all through the first movie? Unless you didn't see *Star Wars*, in which case, why are you still reading this?

Anyway, George comes up to me the first day of filming

and he takes one look at the dress and says, "You can't wear a bra under that dress."

So, I say, "Okay, I'll bite. Why?"

And he says, "Because . . . there's no underwear in space."

I promise you this is true, and he says it with such conviction too! Like he had been to space and looked around and he didn't see any bras or panties or briefs anywhere.

Now, George came to my show when it was in Berkeley. He came backstage and explained why you can't wear your brassiere in other galaxies, and I have a sense you will be going to outer space very soon, so here's why you cannot wear your brassiere, per George. So, what happens is you go to space and you become weightless. So far so good, right? But then your body expands??? But your bra doesn't—so you get strangled by your own bra. Now I think that this would make for a fantastic obit— so I tell my younger friends that no matter how I go, I want it reported that I drowned in moonlight, strangled by my own bra.

But George actually does have a point, because you know when they send out those space probes and they beam back footage of what it looks like up there? All those films ever show are sand and rocks. I've never seen a bra in any of that footage.

So instead of a bra, what do you think I wore for support, intergalactically?

Gaffer's tape.

I used to think there should have been a contest at the end of the day for who in the crew would get to help remove the tape.

Well, I was just thinking of others. Even then. I was just giving, giving, giving.

But clearly, they've gone as far as they can go with this whole doll thing. I mean, what are they going to do next? Make a life-size Leia doll? A kind of Stepford Leia? Which would render me obsolete. You'd read her book. So, thank God they haven't done that. And thank God they haven't come up with a life-size Leia sex doll. Because that would be truly humiliating. Thank God that they haven't made an $800 sex doll that you can put in your cornfield to chase away crows. Oh, wait, they have!

Okay, I admit, I knew about this, and I have to say it does turn out to be kind of a useful thing. Because if ever anyone tells me to go fuck myself, I can actually get the doll and give it a whirl. Well, this actually happened one night at my show. Someone from the far balcony screamed, "Go fuck yourself, Carrie!" So I had the crew load the doll up into my car and I took it back to my hotel and I have to tell you, I spent hours. But here's the thing I have to point out. The doll is cement. Now I don't know how erotic that is for you, but it just doesn't do it for me . . . anymore. Anyway, at about 3:30 A.M. I tried to get the doll to do something with her hand, and it just fell off. So finally at about 4:00 A.M., I think, oh my God, epiphany! The doll is heterosexual. But I really have no way of proving this theory because I no longer have a penis. It is being revoked until the financial crisis is over.

6
"FROM WHAT I CAN SEE OF THE PEOPLE LIKE ME, WE GET BETTER BUT WE NEVER GET WELL"

—PAUL SIMON

Years ago, there were tribes that roamed the earth, and every tribe had a magic person. Well, now, as you know, all the tribes have dispersed, but every so often you meet a magic person, and every so often, you meet someone from your tribe. Which is how I felt when I met Paul Simon.

Paul and I had the secret handshake of shared sensibility. We understood each other perfectly. Obviously we didn't always agree, but we understood the terms of our disagreements.

My mother used to say, "You know dear, Paul can be very charming—when he wants to be."

And my father just wanted Paul to write an album for him.

Anyway, Paul and I dated for six years, were married for two, divorced for one, and then we had good memories of each other and so what do you think we did?

No—no, we didn't remarry. We dated again. Which is exactly what you want to do after you've been married and divorced.

Samuel Johnson once said that remarrying (and he's not talking about marrying the same person here, just remarrying) is the "triumph of hope over experience." So for me, remarrying the same person is the triumph of nostalgia over judgment.

So Paul and I were together for over twelve years (off and on) and we traveled to a bunch of places—all over the world really. And the last place we went to was the Amazon, which I highly recommend by the way—if you like mosquitoes. Anyway, when we got back, Paul wrote an album based on South American music called

The Rhythm of the Saints—and on this album is the last song he ever wrote about me—and it's called "She Moves On." (An ironic title.) If you can get Paul Simon to write a song about you, *do it.* Because he is so brilliant at it. Anyway, one of the lyrics in that song goes like this:

She is like a top / She cannot stop . . .

So yeah, he knew me.

But the lyric I really wanted to tell you about was this:

And I'm afraid that I'll be taken / Abandoned and forsaken / In her cold coffee eyes . . .

Yup, I'm a bitch.

Now, Paul didn't just write unpleasant songs about me.

She's come back to tell me she's gone / As if I didn't know that / As if I didn't know my own bed / As if I didn't notice the way she brushed her hair from her forehead

See? Recognize me now?

He wrote other nice things about me and our time together, but you know how with exes you tend to remember more of the negative things rather than the positive ones?

No? I guess it's only me then.

He wrote another song called "Allergies." And the lyric in that was:

... my heart is allergic / To the woman I love / And it's changing the shape of my face ...

Do you think that's flattering? I don't think it really is.

But Paul also wrote another album—a beautiful album— of course they're all beautiful, but this particular one was called *Hearts and Bones*, and the title song, "Hearts and Bones," was about us . . . and it went like this:

One and one-half wandering Jews / Returned to their natural coasts / To resume old acquaintances / Step out occasionally / And speculate who had been damaged the most ...

But that couldn't be it because I didn't get permission to reprint those lyrics. So that would be really bad, wouldn't it?

Oh, it isn't really bad, because I didn't take any alimony from Paul. So try to think of this as you reading my alimony. And lovely alimony it is.

—*One and one half wandering Jews . . . speculate who had been damaged the most.*

Guess who won that contest?

Poor Paul. He had to put up with a lot with me. I think ultimately I fell under the heading of: *Good Anecdote, Bad Reality.* I was really good for material, but when it came to day-to-day living, I was more than he could take.

We once had a fight (on our honeymoon) where I said, "Not only do I not like you, I don't *like you personally!*" We tried to keep the argument going after that but we were laughing too hard.

So, I married Paul at twenty-six, we divorced when I was twenty-eight, and at twenty-nine I went into rehab. Not because I needed it, but because I was doing research for my novel *Postcards from the Edge*, and I needed to meet some real drug addicts and alcoholics, to give the book some veracity.

7
SADNESS SQUARED

O kay, have it your way, I'm a drug addict.

You know how they say that religion is the opiate of the masses? Well, I took masses of opiates religiously.

But you can't chalk it up to my goofy childhood. You can try, but you'll have a hard time because my brother, Todd, coincidentally, had the same exact childhood and, freakishly, the same parents, but Todd has *never* had a substance abuse problem. So it's not what you're given, it's how you take it. My brother is, however, Born Again Christian. But, what I like to say about that is—what father could Todd find who was more famous than Eddie Fisher—but who he could talk to everyday? Because you can—

(Oh, Jesus.)

Now, I'd always written—ever since I was about fourteen. You know—poems and journals and stuff like that. But when I was twenty-eight, I was interviewed for *Esquire* magazine—you know, *Enquirer, Esquire*, give me a choir I'm there—and the interview turned out funny I guess. I mean, it had one-liners in it like "instant gratification takes too long."

Anyway, a publishing house saw the interview and liked it, so they wrote me a letter asking if I wanted to write a book.

And the letter was forwarded to me in the rehab. And I was glad to get mail from *anyone*.

But I did—I did want to write a book, and I knew what the first line would be: "Maybe I shouldn't have given the guy who pumped my stomach my phone number, but he'll never call me anyway. No one will ever call me again."

And this was based on a true thing. See, the doctor that pumped my stomach sent me flowers. With a note that read: "I can tell that you are a very warm and sensitive person."

All that from the contents of my stomach! I was tempted to marry him so I could tell people how we met.

Anyway, I wrote *Postcards from the Edge* in Los Angeles when I was twenty-eight, and then I got back together with Paul again, so I wrote the screenplay for *Postcards* in New York. Then they started filming the movie in Los Angeles with Meryl Streep and Shirley MacLaine! Well, I want to be on that set. So I started flying out to LA from New York a lot—and this was really bad for my relationship with Paul, and pretty soon we both knew it was over. (He might have known a little sooner than I did.) Mike Nichols used to say we were two flowers, no gardener. No one was minding the relationship.

One time when I was flying back to LA—one of the last times—Paul and I had been fighting all morning, so he drove me to the airport to get rid of me faster and as I was about to get on the plane, I turned to him and said, "You'll feel bad if I crash."

And he shrugged and said, "Maybe not."

Oh, and around that time I got a call from my business office that Bob Dylan wanted my phone number.

And I said, *"Fuck you. You get that stalker away from me. I don't want anymore sixties icons fucking up my life!"*

That's what I said in my head.

Out loud I said, "Absolutely. I'll be waiting by the phone."

Dylan wasn't calling to ask me on a date. He was calling because this cologne company had contacted him to see if he would endorse a cologne called Just Like a Woman. Now Bob didn't like that name, but he liked the idea of endorsing a cologne. And he wanted to know if I had any good cologne names.

Do I look like someone who would be wandering around with a bunch of cologne names rattling around in my head?

Well, tragically, I did. I did have quite a few ideas for cologne names and so I told them to Bob.

There was Ambivalence, for the scent of confusion.

Arbitrary for the man who doesn't give a shit how he smells!

And Empathy—feel like them and smell like *this*.

Well, Bob actually liked those! And then he said he thought he might like to open a beauty salon, and I said, "What? Like Tangled Up and Blown?"

Anyway, a couple of weeks later, I saw George Harrison at this dinner party, as one does, so I tell him that Bob called and he said, "Don't worry, because you know whenever Bob is on the road for a long time, he starts thinking about finding a regular job. You know, a job that will take him off the road."

It turns out that Bob had phoned George the week before to see if he wanted to open The Traveling Wilburys Hotel.

So, a short time after this, I invite Bob to a party at my house, and he arrives with his girlfriend (who was my neighbor at the time) and he's wearing a parka with sunglasses.

And I say, "Thank *God* you wore that, Bob, because sometimes late at night here the sun gets really, really, bright and then it snows."

Later, at the party, I introduce Bob to Meryl Streep, and he takes her hand and says, "Oh, yeah, I know you. You were great in—"

And while he's holding her hand, she now has to go through what turned out to be basically all of her movies, which takes a while, because his favorite turns out to be—*Ironweed.*

My mother doesn't always come to my parties. She doesn't have to really, because she's right next door and can listen to them from across the driveway.

But she has always been there for me.

I mean, obviously she was upset about my drug addiction—what mother wouldn't be. But on some level she wasn't as upset as she was with my failure to do a nightclub act.

Well, that, and dating an agent. She grounded me for weeks when she found out about that. But when he ended up allegedly fathering her extraordinary granddaughter, Billie, all was forgiven.

One of my dozens of psychiatrists once told me that it's important to be able to distinguish the difference between a problem and an inconvenience. The *Oxford English Dictionary* defines a problem as a thing thrown or put forward; hence a question propounded for solution, a set task, a difficult or puzzling question proposed for solution. The first use of the word was in 1382—so I suppose prior to that there was either no way to put a name to one's difficulties—or everyone lived in a world of different levels of inconvenience. Then, after 1382, problemizing could be the order of the day. An inconvenience, on the other hand, is defined as being troublesome—this was in the mid-1600s so I imagine there were three hundred years of problems between 1382 and 1656.

But no matter what the dictionary says, in my opinion, a problem derails your life and an inconvenience is not being able to get a nice seat on the un-derailed train. Given that, I've had three and a half problems. A dead guy in my bed, substance abuse, and manic-depression. My final little problem-ette stems from the difficulty I seem to have in romantic relationships. Specifically, I'm referring to the last categorically "serious" relationship I had; I was left by a man for a man. Billie's father left me for a man named Scott when she was one year old (making Scott the man who got the man who got away).

Anyway, armed with my understanding between a problem and an inconvenience, I realize I've been blessed with very few problems in my life. Let's face it, to complain about my childhood or even a sizeable portion of my life would be as unattractive as it would be inaccurate. I had a very privileged life growing up. A beautiful, loving, eccentric mother; an even-tempered—and consequently odd to me—bright, kind, religious brother; a charming, handsome, womanizing yet virtually absent father; lovely grandparents; and a series of dogs and a bird. I mean I had it all. Which is to say a hearty mix of good and not so hot like so many people.

Right after I got sober (the first time), an interviewer asked me if I was happy, and I said, "Among other things."

Happy is one of the many things I'm likely to be over the course of a day and certainly over the course of a lifetime. But I think if you have the expectation that you're going to be happy throughout your life—more to the point, if you have a need to be comfortable all the time—well, among other things, you have the makings of a classic drug addict or alcoholic. Which is obviously what I became. But actually, through therapy and exposure to the wisdom found in twelve-step programs and beyond, I've gotten an enormous portion of my compulsion for comfort under control.

One night I had to go to a meeting—this three-hour meeting I've gone to every week for the last ten years. (By the way, no, I haven't stayed sober that long, but my failure to achieve long-term sobriety is just that—*my* failure—not the failure of "the program.") I first started going to meetings when I was twenty-eight, but it was at this particular three-hour meeting that I heard someone say that I didn't have to like meetings, I just had to go to them. Well this was a revelation to me! I thought I had to like everything I did. And for me to like everything I did meant—well, among other things, that I needed to take a boat load of dope. Which I did for many, many years. But if what this person told me were true, then I didn't have to actually be comfortable all the time. If I could, in fact, learn to experience a quota of discomfort, it would be awesome news. And if I could consistently go to that three-hour meeting, I could also exercise, and I could write. In short, I could actually be responsible.

But I didn't learn this until after three of my three-and-a-half problems had occurred—the overdose, the bipolar diagnosis, and the man that got the man that got away.

It seemed like a lot of my trouble showed up in sex, it being the alleged road to love and all. In almost—well, I won't say every other situation, but in a lot of situations, you can hardly tell that there is anything really wrong with me—I just have basically too much personality for one person and not quite enough for two. But in the area of romance, Boom!—you know right away.

When I was little—about seven, I guess—I remember getting in the car with my mother when she picked me up from school and telling her that I'd seen the word "fuck" written on the handball court at the playground and I wanted to know what it meant.

And she said, "I'll have to tell you later, dear—when I can draw you diagrams." Well, needless to say "later" never came and neither did—I'm sorry to report—those promised diagrams. Which is a shame, really, because I think they would've come in pretty handy from time to time. Armed with my mother's diagrams I might've moved through the world of dating in smooth easy motions, like a queen, with that straight-backed certainty that comes with being entitled, cared for, and wearing crowns. But without those diagrams—I shuffle around like some street person, clumsy and stooped with the carriage of someone who picks through the trash, shopping for dinner.

But let's face it, the world of sex is weird no matter how you look at it. I mean—fourteen hours after you've had your face smashed into someone's genitals, you're walking down the street with the boy as though that were all "just fine, thank you, how are you!"

The first crush I ever had was on a boy called Willie Breton. For some reason, my friends and I used to try to say his name without using our tongues, which for whatever reason, was highly enjoyable. I can't recommend it as an activity highly enough. Feel free to try it when you're really bored.

Anyway, as it happens, Willie is now an orthodox rabbi living in Israel with his wife and ten children.

How often have I wistfully thought to myself, "Ahhh, if I played my carnal cards right that could've been me . . ."

—Actually, never.

Many years later, when I was in Jerusalem on my honeymoon with Paul, we met up with Willie (now-Rabbi Willie) and his wife for lunch. Willie and Paul fought ceaselessly—largely about the deportation of the Arabs from the West Bank (Rabbi Willie for; Rabbi Paul against). I never realized how fun it could be to get a current partner and a past partner together and then pit them against each other. I mean, if you can't find a good book to read.

Ultimately Paul and I went our separate ways. He went on to marry someone much younger than he was (twenty-five years) and from the south (Edie Brickell), and so, not to be outdone, I found myself a mate younger than *myself* (four years) and also from the south. The only difference between our two choices . . . well, was that his was a girl and mine was a boy, but my choice forgot to tell me he was gay. Well, he forgot to tell me, and I forgot to notice. Hey, it could happen—you know when you're first in love and you're grinning at each other like goofballs and making out all the time (everything looks better when you're infatuated, doesn't it?) like it's lit from within and you're telling each other everything like "I'm a Libra . . . I like fireflies on a warm summer night . . . I like long moonlit walks on the beach on acid—oh, did I forget to tell you I was gay?"

"I should have had a V8!"

Actually, he told me later that I had turned him gay . . . by taking codeine again.

And I said, "You know, I *never* read that warning on the label."

I thought it said *heavy machinery*, not homosexuality—turns out I could have been driving those tractors all along!

Turning people gay is kind of a superpower of mine. It's not called upon a lot, but when it is, I pick up my little pink phone, I put on my rainbow-colored cape, and I'm there like a shot!

You know, I was probably turning people gay for a long, long, *long* time without even knowing it. Because I took a lot of codeine—and I traveled. So there are probably pockets of homosexual communities all over the world started by me. You may have seen some of my handiwork.

My doctor told me that codeine stays in your liver for seven years. I mean unless you have a good lawyer. Well, I don't. I do not have a good lawyer, so what I'm trying to say is, there's probably still some codeine in my liver. So, if you find yourself on your knees in front of someone of the same sex—nude—and that's not where you usually hang out . . . Happy Chanukkah from all of us at "Wishful Drinking"!

8 BRISK AS A BULLET SHOT THROUGH THE CENTER OF EVERYTHING

I was probably rebounding from Paul when I met Bryan (a week later), but Bryan is really, *really* attractive.

When I met him, he had hair. Actually, I do that, too—I make them bald, I turn them gay, my work is done!

But, Bryan took really, really good care of me, and this was the first time a man had ever done that. You know, my father left when I was two (oh, poor, sad Carrie!), and Paul and I were the two-flower thing, so this was the first time a man had ever taken care of me. I mean, he used to give me baths (like I was a Labrador).

Bryan took such good care of me that I thought, "this guy will make a good father." And I was right, he made a great father—and he still does. So fearing now that finally everything would be all right, nine months later our daughter was dragged from my body as though it was a burning building. And once this well-fed, round creature was rescued from the rubble of me, I sent out a birth announcement which read:

Someone's summered in my stomach,
Someone's fallen through my legs,
To make an infant omelet,
Simply scramble sperm and eggs.

So, Bryan and I named our adorable omelet Billie. Billie Catherine Lourd. So, a year later when Bryan left me for Scott—well naturally, I was devastated. I loved Bryan—and I really liked those baths. But my mother was fantastic to me during this time. I mean, my mother . . . she's . . . well, she's like a mother to me and she said this great thing.

She said, "You know, dear, we've had every sort of man in our family—we've had horse thieves and alcoholics and one-man bands—but this is our *first* homosexual!"

Anyway, having nothing to do with Bryan, about a year after that, I was invited to go to a mental hospital. And you know, you don't want to be rude, so you go. Okay, I know what you must be thinking—but this is a very exclusive invitation.

I mean, hello—have you ever been invited to a mental hospital?

So, you see, it's very exclusive. It's sort of like an invitation to the White House—only you meet a better class of people in the mental hospital.

My diagnosis was manic-depression. I think today they call it bipolar—so you might say I swing both ways. But unless you say it really, really loud, I probably won't hear you.

Oh! Before I forget! My mother wants you all to know this comes from my father's side. She's as normal as the day is long.

But imagine this though. Imagine having a mood system that functions essentially like weather—independently of whatever's going on in your life. So the facts of your life remain the same, just the emotional fiction that you're responding to differs. It's like I'm not properly insulated—so all the bad and the good ways that you and most of the people in adjacent neighborhoods and around the world feel—that pours directly into my system unchecked. It's so fun. I call it "getting on my grid" or ESP: Egregious Sensory Protection.

But ultimately I feel I'm very sane about how crazy I am.

But periodically I do explode. Now the good thing about this is that over time, the explosions have gotten smaller and the recovery time is faster, but what is guaranteed is that I will explode. So what I do, because I'm a good hostess (except for the Greg thing)—I provide my guests with bibs. So they don't get my crazy juice all over their nice clothes.

You know how most illnesses have symptoms you can recognize? Like fever, upset stomach, chills, whatever. Well, with manic-depression, it's sexual promiscuity, excessive spending, and substance abuse—and that just sounds like a fantastic weekend in Vegas to me!

Oh! This'll impress you—I'm actually in the *Abnormal Psychology* textbook. Obviously my family is so proud. Keep in mind though, I'm a PEZ dispenser *and* I'm in the *Abnormal Psychology* textbook. Who says you can't have it all?

But when I was told about the textbook, I was told I was in there with a photo.

And I said, "Huh? What photo???"

It's not like anyone ever called me and said, "Have you got a little snapshot of yourself looking depressed or manic?" (Like from my show, for example.)

So for years I wondered—what picture?

Well, I have excellent news. Recently I found the picture, and rather than describing it to you, would you like to see it? Because I really want to show it to you.

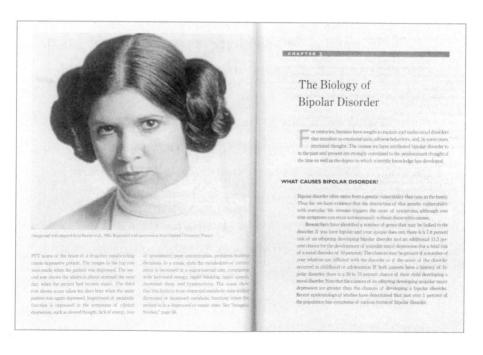

115

So I'm not crazy, *that* bitch is. Anyone who would wear a hairstyle like that *has* to be nuts! Right?

Having received word at an early age that the rest of my life was going to be challenging (at least at very odd intervals), I started seeing a shrink when I was fifteen. The first was recommended to me by Joan Hacket, and he was a psychologist and not a psychiatrist. (Psychiatrists are medical doctors as well as the rest of the psycho stuff. So they're better trained to diagnose mental illness and—oh so much more importantly—prescribe medication for it.) In any case (so to speak), this doctor failed to diagnose my manic depression. Though one day, after I'd been seeing him for many years, he suddenly asked if I'd been hyperactive as a child. Yeah, right . . . and I'd just somehow forgotten to mention a little thing like that. I mean, it wasn't as if I had an endless supply of life struggles to discuss with him at that point. Although surely adolescence is a struggle in and of itself—but not so much so that I'd somehow forgotten to mention my hyperactivity. But I think that my first doctor saw something in me that was amiss but as to what that something was, for that moment, would remain a mystery.

My second doc knew exactly what was up (and down) with me. And though generally it's useless to diagnose someone as bipolar who is engaged in ingesting large quantities of drugs or alcohol—which I was— because drug addiction and alcoholism, done properly of course, classically mimics the symptoms of manic-depression.

So when I was twenty-four years old, Dr. Barry Stone told me that it was his utterly professional opinion that I was hypomanic, also known as bipolar one, which is the lesser version of manic depression—excessively moody—as opposed to bipolar two—excruciatingly moody, which includes the occasional hallucination and lockup ward visits. As it turns out, I was ultimately determined to be the latter (excruciatingly moody) but from where old Doc Stone sat, I was simply excessively moody. Hey, maybe the whole show hadn't kicked in yet. Or better still, maybe the drugs were suppressing my symptoms to a certain extent.

I mean, that's at least in part why I ingested chemical waste—it was a kind of desire to abbreviate myself. To present the CliffsNotes of the emotional me, as opposed to the twelve-volume read.

I used to refer to my drug use as putting the monster in the box. I wanted to be less, so I took more—simple as that. Anyway, I eventually decided that the reason Dr. Stone had told me that I was hypomanic was that he wanted to put me on medication instead of actually treating me. So I did the only rational thing I could do in the face of such an insult—I stopped talking to the Stone, flew back to New York, and married Paul Simon a week later.

Jump-cut to two years after that and you'll find me overdosing. Not that that was my intention by any means—that was simply the amount of drugs that had become necessary for me to take to get where I wanted to go. My destination being, simply, anywhere but here. But somehow en route to that numb place, I'd overshot my mark and almost arrived at nowhere but dead. Well after that happened, I was quite naturally upset and terrified. I had in no way intended to risk my life. I just wanted to turn the sound down and smooth all of my sharp corners. Block out the dreadfully noisy din of not being good enough—which on occasion I was actually able to do.

But how had I managed to end up at the destination of dead when that was never the direction I originally set off in? It's as if I tripped and almost fell into my own grave. My only intent was to feel better—which is to say, not to feel at all.

So based on the fact that my best thinking got me in an emergency room with a tube down my throat, I had no trouble at all accepting the fact that I was an alcoholic. Not that I drank all that much—you might say I took pills alcoholically. Anyway, I didn't have any difficulty accepting the notion that my life had become unmanageable. I mean, let's face it, my most creative achievement at that time was having unnecessary gum surgery just for the morphine. (I don't think you can use the word "just" and "morphine" anywhere near each other.) So I threw myself into twelve-step group recovery—believing now that alcoholism was the headline, the overriding thing wrong with me. Which was, of course, in large part true and remains true to this day.

Because I have to admit (well, I don't *have* to . . .), periodically I have had drug slips. All in, I've had about four or five slips since I first started going to twelve-step support groups at the age of twenty-eight. Making that four or five slips in twenty-three years, which is not great. I mean, I'm not proud that I wasn't able to remain sober that entire time—especially in terms of my daughter, who has had to suffer the most from these largely inexcusable forays back down the dark path that is drug use. The most painful thing about returning to this dark planet is seeing the look of disappointment and hurt that these forays invariably put in the eyes of your loved ones. But ultimately you could say that I don't have a problem with drugs so much as I have a problem with sobriety. And it wasn't Alcoholics Anonymous that failed me—it's that I have, on occasions, failed them by not working what they call a good program. But I keep going back. I'm as addicted to all the things A.A. has to offer as I am to the things that made me need those groups in the first place.

But when I first got to twelve-step land—after my stomach pumping incident—I thought, Okay, fine then, this is what the matter is with me. I'm not going to shrinks anymore. My best shrinking and thinking got me into emergency rooms all over Southern California. So I planned to be an all-meeting-all-the-time gal. Psychiatrists were a thing of the past. Why, they hadn't even told me I was an alcoholic! So screw them—especially the doctor who tried to convince me I was hypomanic. Huh! Fat lot he knew. Well, as it turned out, what he knew was an extremely fat lot after all because over the next year of getting and staying clean and sober all the people I'd come into the program with were calming down and leveling out while I seemed to be doing just the opposite. Quick to excite, to agitate, to engage, to anger—I was heading straight up into the rafters of my overly good or bad time.

In short—okay, fine, yes, I know it's far too late for that—I was manic, the monster was out of the box, the cat was out of the bag, and it appeared after a year of erratic sobriety that I was en route back to the shrinks and psychopharmacologists I imagined myself not needing anymore. Without the substances, I had used to distort and mask my symptoms, it was now all too clear that I was a bona fide, wild-ride manic-depressive. And this initially dismaying discovery led me to my third and best shrink, Beatriz Foster, who turned out to be the psychiatrist who finally got me to address my manic-depression.

And I ultimately not only addressed it, I named my two moods Roy and Pam. Roy is Rollicking Roy, the wild ride of a mood, and Pam is Sediment Pam, who stands on the shore and sobs. (Pam stands for "piss and moan.") One mood is the meal, and the next mood is the check.

There are a couple of reasons why I take comfort in being able to put all this in my own vernacular and present it to you. For one thing, because then I'm not completely alone with it. And for another, it gives me a sense of being in control of the craziness. Now this is a delusion, but it's *my* delusion and I'm sticking with it. It's sort of like: I have problems but problems don't have me.

Statistics say that a range of mental disorders affects more than one in four Americans in any given year. That means millions of people are totally batshit.

But having perused the various tests available that they use to determine whether you're manic depressive, OCD, schizo-affective, schizophrenic, or whatever, I'm surprised the number is that low. So I have gone through a bunch of the available tests, and I've taken questions from each of them, and assembled my own psychological evaluation screening which I thought I'd share with you.

So, here are some of the things that they ask to determine if you're mentally disordered. If you say yes to any number of these questions, you, too, could be insane.

1. In the last week, have you been feeling irritable?
2. In the last week, have you gained a little weight?
3. In the last week, have you felt like not talking to people?
4. Do you no longer get as much pleasure doing certain things as you used to?

5. In the last week, have you felt fatigued?

6. Do you think about sex a lot?

If you don't say yes to any of these questions either you're lying, or you don't speak English, or you're illiterate, in which case, I have the distinct impression that I may have lost you quite a few chapters ago.

9 AN ALTERED, FALTERING SELF

Now, come back with me to when I was first told that I was an alcoholic—which greatly relieved me by the way, because I knew *something* was the matter with me, so I thought, "Great! That's it—that's what I've been struggling with (and enjoying) all this time! Fantastic!"

But what they further do—to (I think) soften the blow of this arguably awkward new way of looking at yourself—they enumerate a number of other famous and accomplished folks who have also struggled with (and enjoyed) alcoholism.

There was:

Scott Fitzgerald

Mel Gibson

Dylan Thomas

Ireland

Rush Limbaugh

Lindsay Lohan

Russia

And George W. Bush

I think their point is—don't feel bad, you're joining an illustrious group. Great people have been alcoholics. Oh, be one, it's fun!

Now I don't think they're implying you could be great, but those people weren't exactly losers (except probably to some members of their families, and all of their constituents) so relax and join the great drunks who staggered the Earth before you.

So, when I was told I was a manic-depressive, there was a whole new list waiting for me.

There was Abraham Lincoln—who wrote the Gettysburg Address in four hours—now that's pretty manic

Winston Churchill, who called his depressed mood the black dog

Korea

Kristy McNichol and Sir Isaac Newton (who I think
would have made an adorable couple!)

Mark Twain

St. Francis

St. Theresa

Jonathan Winters

Poor Brittany Spears

And George W. Bush

Well, naturally after this list I felt invigorated—but
then that is part of my diagnosis.

So, to celebrate my newfound ascent into the lofty
heights of this noble group, I thought I would inau-
gurate a Bipolar Pride Day. You know, with floats and
parades and stuff! On the floats we would get the de-
pressives, and they wouldn't even have to leave their
beds—we'd just roll their beds out of their houses, and
they could continue staring off miserably into space.
And then for the manics, we'd have the manic march-
ing band, with manics laughing and talking and shopping and fucking and making bad judgment calls.

Of course, all this is still in the early planning
stages—and knowing manics it probably always will
be—but the point is we have a plan and that's what

counts. Because when you're manic, every urge is like an edict from the Vatican. No plan is a bad one, because if you're there and you're doing it, it can't be bad. It's like a bank error in your favor.

Mania is, in effect, liquid confidence . . . when the tide comes in, it's all good. But when the tide goes out, the mood that cannot and should not be named comes over you and into you. Because to name it would be an act of summoning.

Losing your mind is a frightening thing—especially if you have a lot to lose—but once it's lost, it's fine! No big deal! There could be a light shining out of your head. It's sort of like glowing in your own dark.

Part of my story—because God forbid you miss a minute of it—is that I stayed awake for six days. This happened because two of my medications were interacting badly, so the doctors put me on what they called a medication vacation—now on a vacation like this you don't get a tan, there is no Club Med, and you can't send cute little postcards. Now, anyone who has stayed awake for six days knows that there's every chance that they'll wind up psychotic. Anyway, I did, and part of how that manifested was that I thought everything on television was about me.

Now if anything like this should happen to you, I

have some excellent advice. Don't watch CNN. Please. Watch one of those pet training shows or cooking shows—even some of the discovery shows might be okay. But I watched CNN, and at the time Versace had just been killed by that man Cunanin, and the police were frantically scouring the Eastern seaboard for him. So I was Cunanin, Versace, and the Police. Now this is exhausting programming.

But by the time I got to be Versace, he was dead. And also by then I was in the *real* hospital part of Cedars-Sinai hospital in Los Angeles, and I could literally hear the nurses outside of the door saying, "Don't listen to her, she's crazy."

My brother eventually arrived and he had to call the mental hospital to see about getting me in because there was, as my friend Dave says, "no room at the bin." You had to be seriously nuts to qualify for residence in the lockdown ward. So finally, the head doctor of the facility came over. This guy looked like this kind of weird John Steinbeck character with his abnormally high pants and his strangely neat hair and his trimmed just so beard.

So he walks in, and I say, "Finally, here's someone who can tell us what it's like to get his cock sucked."

Because (as you might have noticed) I had begun

swearing a lot and apparently I couldn't stop. Something in me had become unleashed and taming it was not imminent.

Anyway, this was my audition for the locked ward, and, as you probably guessed by now, I passed. I made it into the mental hospital. Hurray!

When you qualify for the mental hospital, you have to sign yourself in, like commitment papers, I guess; but I was so far gone I didn't know what I was signing or doing, and so when they put the papers in front of me, I took the pen and I signed with my left hand, "Shame."

That's how I signed in for the mental hospital. How sad is that?

Oh, and my form of mental illness is also a tiny bit infectious by the way. I may have gotten it from Amy Winehouse's toilet seat. So, by the end of this book you could be gay *and* insane! Unless you began that way.

Anyway, ever since my fateful announcement on Diane Sawyer that I was mentally ill—like anyone really needed to know that. Don't you hate it when celebrities just blah blah blah—talk about themselves—I mean, who asked?—I find it all so wearying . . .

Anyway, where was I? So having waited my entire life to get an award for something, anything (okay fine, not acting, but what about a tiny little award for writing? Nope), I now get awards all the time for being mentally ill. I'm apparently very good at it and am honored for it regularly. Probably one of the reasons I'm such a shoo-in is that there's no swimsuit portion of the competition.

Hey, look, it's better than being bad at being mentally ill, right? How tragic would it be to be runner-up for Bipolar Woman of the Year?

The first time I did drugs was when I was thirteen. Before we lost all our money, my family had a vacation house in Palm Springs, about two hours outside of Beverly Hills, where I ostensibly grew up. So periodically my mother used to rent that house in Palm Springs to these people who, after one of their stays, left behind a bag of marijuana. Who knows? Maybe they left it intentionally, a kind of chemical sacrifice on the altar of appreciation for their time there. Anyway, after my mother found the pot, she came to me and said, "Dear, I thought instead of you going outside and smoking pot where you might get caught and get in trouble—I thought you and I might experiment with it together."

Well, frankly at the time, and let's face it—even now—I couldn't imagine anything weirder. But what actually came to pass was that after presenting this bizarre, albeit marginally appealing proposal, my mother got swept back up in the whirlwind of her life and promptly forgot about it. But being the crafty, eager-for-the-altered-state person I was destined to become, I absolutely did not. So once it became obvious that our proposed experiment had slipped my mother's mind, I snuck into the lab of her sacheted underwear drawer and stole the pot, subsequently experimenting my brains out in my backyard tree house with my friend May—who coincidentally also ended up in A.A.!

And you've got to figure that I enjoyed it, because I ended up experimenting with marijuana for the next six years until it suddenly—and I think rather rudely—turned on me. Where at the onset it was all giggles and munchies and floating in a friendly haze—it suddenly became creepy and dark and scary. What was a junkie to do? Well, the answer was quite obvious—I needed to find a new replacement drug. This was when I was about nineteen, while I was filming *Star Wars*. (It ultimately turned out to be Harrison's pot that did me in.) So, after carefully casting about for a substitute substance, I finally settled into my new drug digs—hallucinogens and painkillers. Mind expanders and painkillers. (Though over time and protracted use their meanings got jumbled until they became mind relievers and pain expanders—a place where everything hurt and nothing made sense.)

Anyway, at a certain point in my early twenties, my mother started to become worried about my obviously ever-increasing drug ingestion. So she ended up doing what any concerned parent would do.

She called Cary Grant.

In case you haven't heard, one of the many things Mr. Grant was known for at the time was the fact that at some point in the sixties he famously did a course of LSD while under a doctor's supervision. It's always been difficult for me to imagine this . . . do they actually drop the acid in the doctor's office? Does the doctor do it too? I always thought there was a kind of strange dignity and an even stranger credibility given to acid done under the cool shade of medical supervision. Sometimes, when I heard the phrase "experimenting with drugs," I imagined someone in a white coat excitedly emerging from a lab carrying a smoking beaker and shouting, "I found it, I found it!" But when I heard that Cary Grant had experimented with acid under the supervision of his doctor, well, in a way it was as if he was dedicating his hallucinogenic jaunt to modern science. I imagined him doing it a little reluctantly and with a quiet dignity. After, of course, washing his hands and putting on one of those backless hospital garbs ten minutes before the medicinal acid kicked in.

Anyway, my concerned and caring mother called Cary Grant and told him that her daughter had a problem with acid. You know, like I was mainlining the stuff. You have to admit though, on a certain level, it was an incredibly darling thing for her to do—especially when you factor in the fact that I *loved* Cary Grant. I still do—only now at more of a distance. He's probably the only famous person I was ever really in awe of. Having two celebrity parents, and a few celebrity boyfriends, it was extremely rare for me to get star struck. Not that I was blasé about famous people—I just wasn't bowled over and tongue-tied and staring, as if I'd just undergone more electroshock therapy or stuck my finger in a socket.

But Cary Grant, well . . . he just killed me. I mean, I was completely blown away by him. He had it all—an easygoing class, quiet confidence, wit—all in this beyond-handsome package. So when the phone rang and a familiar voice informed me that he was Cary Grant—even a Cary Grant that was gonna maybe give me a "just say no" drug lecture—well, initially I was, in fact, totally tongue-tied. Normally, I wouldn't have believed that the person on the other end really was Cary Grant—but when he told me my mother had asked him to call, well that sounded eerily like some bizarre thing my mother would do.

In a way, there was actually a precedent for this Cary Grant intervention call.

Some years prior, I was in London en route to my mother's wedding (I don't like to miss any of my parents' weddings). She called me at the hotel where I was staying, and when I didn't answer the phone she became understandably concerned. So she let the phone ring and ring and ring—until finally she panicked. She knew I was in the room so, in her mind, probably the only reason I wasn't answering the phone was that I had overdosed. So she did what any normal concerned mother might do when troubled about her daughter's well being.

She called Ava Gardner.

And she asks Ava to come to my hotel and get the concierge to let her into my room to make sure I'm not dead.

Anyway, the reason this relates to Cary Grant—if it isn't obvious—is that the Ava Gardner Rescue Squad (good title for a rock band) is the reason I would even *begin* to believe that someone telling me that they were Cary Grant might actually in fact *be* Cary Grant. So initially when I got on the phone with Mr. Grant, I was incredibly nervous seeing as how I was on the phone with no less then my fucking hero, but once we began to discuss my acid addiction, after a freakishly short time I found myself chatting gaily with what might as well have been a Cary Grant impersonator. (Because let's face it, there was no actual visual confirmation that this was, in fact, Cary Grant.) So I think I finally convinced him that, despite my mother's insistence, I didn't have an acid problem (which, for the most part, was true). What I *did* have was an opiate problem, but frankly that was none of Cary Grant's fucking business. No matter how much I admired him.

Anyway, though we chatted for about an hour or so, I have basically no memory of what we discussed. Oh yes, there was one thing . . . Chevy Chase and how he had insinuated on some talk show that Mr. Grant was bisexual. Now, as it happened, I was working on a film with Chevy at that time (a marvelous film called *Under the Rainbow*— a riveting film about the making of the *Wizard of Oz*— starring Chevy, me, Eve Arden, and three thousand dwarves), and Chevy and I were getting along somewhat less than a house on fire. So on top of our LSD chat, we had that in common. Poor Chevy Chase relations. So when our hour-long chat was up, I bid Mr. Grant a grateful good-bye, gleefully told all my friends, and end of story. Now, I thought, I had a Cary Grant story to tell my children and grandchildren for years to come. Right?

Well, as it turned out, actually no—not right—because

my Cary Grant story continued and this time from an unexpected direction.

A few years later my father went to Princess Grace's funeral in Monaco.

Please ask me if he actually knew the princess. Of course he didn't. My father had never even met the woman—either prior to her ascent to the throne when she was "just" plain old Grace Kelly, the Oscar-winning movie star or after she became Monaco's very own royal highness.

But I learned that you don't actually have to know the person whose funeral you're attending. In fact, sometimes, depending on the person, it's better that way, but my father had his own reasons for going to the funeral for this very famous, beautiful woman. Publicity.

So there's my father wandering around aimlessly at this far-flung funeral of a famous woman—one of the few beautiful women of his generation that he hadn't slept with—shmoozing with the thousands of other mourners, trying to make eye contact with someone who he could grieve with and maybe generate a photo op in the process, when he spies Cary Grant. And something clicked in his brain and that something turned out to be the dim recollection of a story he'd only just recently been told.

What was it again? Oh yeah—something to do with his first-born daughter.

By now he's walked up to my hero and he says the first thing that pops into his head, which is something along the lines of "My daughter Carrie is addicted to acid, and I'm very worried about her. Would you mind maybe having a talk with her?"

Great. I've now gone from having an acid problem straight to a full-on LSD addiction (as if such a thing were possible). I'm mainlining the stuff.

So here we go again. Poor Cary Grant (I'm sure he's very rarely been called that) gets back from the funeral and in due course calls me again to discuss my issue with slamming acid.

Well, if I was embarrassed the first time he called me, this time I was completely humiliated. I explain to Mr. Grant, after thanking him profusely for taking the time out to counsel me on my alleged dependence on hallucinogens, that, in fact, I didn't spend all that much time with my father—the time required to be able to accurately ascertain as to whether or not I had *any* sort of problem, much less a drug one. I suggest to Mr. Grant that my mother would probably be in a much better position to determine whether or not I was tripping my brain out on a daily basis than my father, who I'd spent, on average, one day a year with.

So Mr. Grant says, "Well, it was very nice of your

father to express his concern. It's very difficult to maintain a relationship with a child after the mother and father have divorced. I have a daughter myself and I see her as much as I can, but when a child divides her time between two houses, no matter how you try it's impossible to spend as much time with your child as you'd like to."

So perhaps my father's motive hadn't been solely to find a subject matter to talk to Cary Grant about at the photo-op funeral. Mr. Grant didn't seem to think so. So maybe this was another example of nothing ever being just one thing. No motive is pure. No one is good or bad—but a hearty mix of both. And sometimes life actually gives to you by taking away.

Anyway, Mr. Grant and I stay on the phone for over an hour talking about this and that—how he wishes he could be a more involved parent—you know, the usual shooting-the-shit-with-Cary-Grant-type thing. It was great.

The phone call eventually comes to a close, and I immediately go to the liquor store and buy him a bottle of wine from his birth year, which is something like 1907, and now he calls me again to thank me.

And in that final phone call, I believe he told me, "I don't even like wine."

I mean, we're ultimately talking about no less than

three calls from Cary Grant. The guy was practically stalking me!

Anyway, cut to a few months later, and I'm at this premiere or charity event or something and I turn and there, just a few feet away from me, actually in the flesh—as far in as you could get—is Cary Grant. Big as life and twice as famous.

But this time it's not just some disembodied voice that sounds a lot like Cary Grant—no, this is the real deal. Classy and handsome and just about everything a human can possibly be when they're a DNA jackpot. But am I intimidated? Oh, my *god*, yes.

So—with my heart pounding in my ears and my nose and my hair, I sheepishly approach my ideal and very timidly tap him on the back, withdrawing my hand immediately as if I burned my finger on his radioactive sizzling hot, iconic back. Whereupon Cary Grant turns, and I immediately start backing away from him, as though one of us was contaminated.

"Hi. I'm Debbie Reynolds's daughter," I admit as though this was a crime. "We talked on the phone?"

I'm stooped over like someone frightened and ashamed.

"Anyway, no big deal—I don't want to bother you—I just wanted to say hi."

"Oh hello, yes. How are you?"

I'm still backing up, forcing him to follow me.

"Oh, I'm fine," I whisper. "Everything's great! Good to see you. Bye!"

And I fled the scene of this social crime, never to return.

Years later, while I was in Australia doing some terrible film, they announced on the radio that Cary Grant had passed away. And I remember getting this pain— the kind you get when you experience a body blow. Or lose something essential.

Who would talk me out of slamming LSD now?

So I think to myself after all this, after all the night clubs and the gay husband and the rehabs (one of my fellow inmates at the last rehab I was in was Ozzie Osbourne . . . that went well!) . . . so, after all the rehabs and all the mental hospitals, I think to myself: If what doesn't kill you makes you—well, what doesn't kill you makes you not dead but if what doesn't kill you makes you stronger, then I should be able to lift Cedars-Sinai Hospital and glow in the dark. So I say to myself at this point—BRING IT ON!!!

Don't *ever* say that. Because it will be brought.

'Cause that's when my friend Greg died.

THE NEWLY MADE BYSTANDER

I didn't realize I actually had post-traumatic stress disorder at the time, but why would I think I had that? Anyway, how would I know which was post-traumatic stress, which is addiction, which is bipolar, which is Libra? Also, I thought you had to go to Iraq to get post-traumatic stress disorder—and you do—but you can also just come on over to my house!

Anyway, a few months later, I guess my friends were getting worried about me because I wasn't talking—and most people know that I'm essentially voice activated—and I was smoking like it was food, so I finally agreed to go to this grief counselor they'd found for me.

And my favorite thing this woman said to me was, "I'm so sorry we had to meet under these conditions."

Hello!? You're a grief counselor! What other conditions would we meet under?

Then she says, "I can't even imagine what you've been through."

You can't!? Well if *you* can't then I'm really fucked.

Anyway, a couple of weeks later, my daughter, Billie, who was about thirteen at the time, tells me that she wants to be a neurologist with a specialty in schizophrenia when she grows up.

So I say, "Why not be a grief counselor? We'll see each other more."

My daughter, Billie, is incredible. Even though she's a teenage girl and they so often end up thinking their moth-

ers are lame and/or insane (and in Billie's case, she's not completely wrong). She's so pretty (she looks a lot like my mother) and she's a straight-A student—except for chemistry and when's that gonna come up? And, she's a great writer and has a wonderful singing voice. (Where'd she get that?) And she just got her driver's license so pray for me.

Anyway, once, when Billie was about four we were driving along in Florida and she sees this church and she points to it and says, "What's that?"

So I said, "Well, baby, that's where people go to worship God."

And she says, "God, like the God Bless You God?"

Like that's his main claim to fame.

I took a job at one point when Billie was about three or four with a magazine who would send me to different places with her and one of her friends and then I would write about it. I wanted to call it "Billie's Holiday," but they ended up cleverly calling it "Travels With Billie." So we got to go to all sorts of places. One time, we went to Vegas and visited my mother's hotel where there were actually slot machines that, in order to win, you had to get three faces in a line of my mother's smiling face but no matter how many times I tried to get a jackpot with my mother's head, I never seemed to be able to win. I couldn't hit the jackpot with my mother's smiling face! If I'd dreamt that, a shrink would have a field day analyzing its deeper meaning.

Billie has always been a very verbal and watchful child. And you know what's terrible nowadays is everything that is on TV and the internet. You know, you get movies that are rated PG or PG-13, but it's not a system that accurately indicates just how sophisticated or explicit these films are. Anyway, one day, Billie and I were watching *Muriel's Wedding*, and I was thinking: Well, this is okay, right? I mean, why shouldn't she see this? I didn't remember it as anything inappropriate, so I'm sitting there with her and suddenly one of the girls in the movie says: "She sucked your husband's cock." And then another woman responds: "Oh, well, she also sucked *your* husband's cock." Now, I'm sitting there next to Billie and I'm devastated. What do I say, if anything? She's about seven at the time.

So I say, "You don't think people actually *do* that, do you?" (Great! There's a brilliant point.)

And she looks sheepish and says, "No." Then about six months later, we're watching yet another one of these movies that I think is totally fine, when it happens again! Another actress makes a reference to going down on a man.

146

So, I say to Billie again, "You don't think people actually *do* that, do you?"

I don't know what she's been exposed to between the internet and school—no matter how diligently I try to monitor it.

But this time she responds very quietly, "Yes."

I'm totally unprepared for this so I say, "But you don't think men actually *like* it, do you?"

And to this, she emphatically shakes her head No.

So, you can see how great I am with training with my daughter. I did tell her about the birds and the bees, but you kind of have to move really fast because of what kids are exposed to now. The weird thing is when kids see porn before they have scx and ugh...well, actually, I'm a fine one to talk because when I was fifteen, I was in the chorus of my mother's show (like most teenagers) and the gay guys in the show showed a movie called *Sixteen Inches in Omaha* to either shock me or watch my reaction.

As you can imagine, this is a wonderful introduction into the male anatomy. So subtle and nuanced.

Anyway, more recently Billie told me that she's changed her mind—she no longer wants to be a neurologist with a specialty in schizophrenia, now she wants to be a comic. (which is kind of a natural progression if you think about it).

So I say, "Well, baby—if you want to be a comic, you have to be a writer. But don't worry, you have *tons* of material. Your mother is a manic-depressive drug addict, your father is gay, your grandmother tap-dances, and your grandfather shot speed!"

And my daughter laughs and laughs and laughs, and I say, "Baby, the fact that you know that's funny is going to save your whole life."

Now, if you had a daughter that great—you don't, but if you did—wouldn't you want to do something nice for her? Well, I did. I wanted her to have some normal Mommy memories of me. Not just memories of a mother who got tattooed and hid Easter eggs in July. So I learned to cook. And it turns out I'm a pretty good cook. I mean, I make most of my meals at about 11:00 at night, but they're very, very delicious!

But when I first learned to cook, my mother flipped out. It was like I was violating a family code or credo— I didn't even know we had those things.

She would say, "Carrie's in the kitchen…*cooking*."

Like she was saying, "shaving her head." And what a weird thing to do in the kitchen, by the way.

So, one night, I'm at her house (I told you we live next door to each other) and I say, "I'm going back up to my house to make Billie dinner."

And she grabs my arm and says "*Nooo!* Why are you doing this?! Please let me send Mary to make her chicken crepes."

But I'm pleased to report that, over time, my mother has become more accustomed to my cooking so now she says, "You know, dear, we had an Uncle Wally in the family who was a good cook."

So, if she can see it as a talent—especially one from her side of the family—she's cool with it.

I heard someone say once that many of us only seem able to find heaven by backing away from hell. And while the place that I've arrived at in my life may not precisely be everyone's idea of heavenly, I could swear sometimes—if I'm quiet enough—I can hear the angels sing.

Either that or I've screwed up my medication. But one of the reasons I think my life is going so much better is that having originally done *Wishful Drinking* (the show and now the book) as a singles ad—a really, really detailed personals ad—I think if I attract someone from one of my audiences or one of the readers of this book, he'll never be able to say, "You never told me you were a manic-depressive drug addict who turned men bald and gay," like men say to me now. Because I am no different than any other single person (all three of them). I also want someone to love and treasure and overwhelm—oh, and disappoint!—especially disappoint, I find that so erotic. Anyway, the ad worked! Because when I did my show in Santa Fe, I received in the mail a marriage proposal.

Now, I told you I was a manic depressive, right? So you know I have lousy judgment—so I was hoping that before I take such an enormous step, I could run the proposal past you and get you to somehow weigh in on it. Okay?

Keep in mind—I'm not getting any younger.

Dearest Carrie Fisher,

I want a relationship with you because I want to get married and have sex every night. [Because that is what you do when you are married.] *You are older than me, but I am a full grown man of forty-one. I do love you Carrie.*

Here are the most personal things about me. I have a big tummy and I had an anus operation for hardened hemorrhoid bleeding. [Which is good to know because now I can never say to him, "You never told me you had an anus operation for a hardened hemorrhoid bleeding!" Like I would.] *I used to buy VHS videos for self-gratification since I was fifteen to a couple of years ago.*

I have had sex before and I'm not a virgin since I was fourteen. I never had a girlfriend or been married because I was seeking stardom for myself until fall of 1992. [Because you all remember what happened in the fall of 1992.]

I love the band Duran Duran and the movie Star Wars *and the TV shows* MacGyver *and* The Price Is Right.

Please feel free to write me.

I love you Carrie.

So, what do you think? Should I marry him? Are you an optimist like Marie McDonald?

Come on, I want to get old *with* someone—not *because* of them—and I already have such a huge head start!

11
A SPY IN THE HOUSE OF ME

Before I wrap up, I'd like to share some of the things with you that I've learned from going through all this nonsense.

- "Resentment is like drinking a poison and waiting for the other person to die."
- Saying you're an alcoholic *and* an addict is like saying you're from Los Angeles *and* from California.
- Some of the wisdom I have gotten from my grandmother—my mother's mother—the closet locker, who taught me, "A fly is as likely to land on shit as it is on pie" (which is true, if you think about it). She also

said, "Cry all you want, you'll pee less!" (I don't know if that is true though.)

- But the main thing I've learned, I learned all by myself, no help needed. I learned not to get my tongue pierced. Because if you're getting it pierced for the reason why I think you're getting it pierced and you're not good at that thing to begin with, no little piece of jewelry is going to save the day.

I was talking to a priest friend of mine recently (as one does) and I was telling him about how I was scheduled to meet with my daughter and her shrink the following week.

"It's going to be so difficult," I moaned.

He shrugged. "You've done difficult before."

Well, who hasn't done difficult before?

As I mentioned earlier, I turned fifty-two this year. (Did you hear, they made an announcement that fifty-two is the new thirty-one—or the new black.)

And I like to think of myself as a threshold guardian. *"There but for the sake of me, go you!"*

If I've forgotten to tell you anything in these pages, it could be the ECT, it could be bad memory from getting old, or it could be because there's just too much stuff stuck in my head.

Sherlock Holmes believed the brain could only hold just so much information, so if he ever learned anything that was useless to his profession, he set about systematically to try to forget it.

I like to quote fictional characters, because I'm something of a fictional character myself! But my point is that I have something stuck in my brain. And because it's in there I frequently get lost on my way to people's houses, I always forget people's names, and I leave stuff everywhere so that my husband, Dick Tater, has to pick up after me. And at times I forget parts of my show, which is how this whole thing got started. So now I've written it down at least.

Anyway, the following is the "something" that I have stuck in my brain which I go about trying to systematically forget publicly here in these pages! (And if you understood that, you're in desperate need of medication.)

It's a poem. Yes, as you probably guessed, a poem, by George Lucas:

General Kenobi, years ago, you served my father in the Clone Wars; now he begs you to help him in his struggle against the Empire. I regret that I am unable to present my father's request to you in person; but my ship has fallen under attack, and my mission to bring you to

Alderaan has failed. I have placed information vital to the survival of the rebellion into the memory systems of this R2 unit. (Proper Copper Coffee Pot.) *My father will know how to retrieve it. You must see this droid safely delivered to him on Alderaan. This is our most desperate hour. Help me, Obi-Wan Kenobi—you're my only hope.*

I can't forget that stupid, fucking hologram speech! That's why I did dope!

NEW YORK

A GUIDE TO THE CITY'S BEST
RESTAURANTS & ENTERTAINMENT

CARRIE FISHER IS BOVINE AND UNAPPEALING,
HAVING INHERITED THE WORST QUALITIES
OF BOTH HER PARENTS - JOHN SIMON

America's Newspaper

ENQUIRER

DEBBIE AND EDDIE BACK TOGETHER

For 2 Minutes Having Run Into
Each Other Shopping Downtown

The New York Times

FRIDAY, MARCH 25, 2005

UNDERWEAR DISCOVERED IN SPACE

GEORGE LUCAS SAYS: "I TOLD YOU SO"

Los Angeles Times

MONDAY, SEPTEMBER 19, 1997

Carrie Fisher Selected As Runner Up
Bipolar Woman Of The Year

AUTHOR'S NOTE

One of the things that baffles me (and there are quite a few) is how there can be so much lingering stigma with regards to mental illness, specifically bipolar disorder. In my opinion, living with manic depression takes a tremendous amount of balls. Not unlike a tour of duty in Afghanistan (though the bombs and bullets, in this case, come from the inside). At times, being bipolar can be an all-consuming challenge, requiring a lot of stamina and even more courage, so if you're living with this illness and functioning at all, it's something to be proud of, not ashamed of.

They should issue medals along with the steady stream of medications one has to ingest.

ACKNOWLEDGMENTS

Thank you to my inextinguishable and amazing mother and neighbor, Debbie.

To my brother, Todd—hogger of all the sanity available in our freak family.

To Greg Stevens, my best and only Republican friend—no one will ever be as much fun to shop with. I miss you every day.

To the epic engineer of all my elsewheres, magician assistant, memory and running mate, Garret Edington.

To Melissa North, South, East, and West—I'd follow you in any direction you decided to travel in.

To my father, Puff Daddy, who gave in part by taking away—thanks for the highest grade of absence available on Earth.

To Josh Ravetch—who helped me get this whole *Wishful Drinking* thing started—I owe you big time.

To Daniel and Marcus and Jamie—the father, son, and Holy Ghost of our heavenly *Wishful Drinking* spiritual tour of America—without your additional care I would be next to nothing and too near to normal to make a name for not only myself, but someone all too nauseatingly like me.

To Clancy Imislund—whose voice is louder than my head—thank you for keeping sobriety fun.

To Helen Fielding—thank you for keeping sanity fun.

To Judy and RJ Cooper, Dave Mirkin, Bruce Wagner, Bruce Cohen, Craig Bierko, Abe Gurko, The Tolkins, Rachel and the Edgars (big and small), Gloria and Mary, Cyndi Sayre, Michael Gonzalez, and my literary mod squad—Suzanne Gluck, Kerri Kolen, and David Rosenthal.

Photo Identifications for Pages 36 and 37

Page 36:

First row (left to right): Eddie Fisher, Debbie Reynolds, Harry Karl, Richard Hamlett

Second row (left to right): Carrie Fisher, Todd Fisher, Marie MacDonald, Connie Stevens

Third row (left to right): Paul Simon, Bryan Lourd, Joely Fisher, Tricia Fisher

Fourth row: Billie Lourd

Page 37:

First row (left to right): Elizabeth Taylor, Mike Todd, Richard Burton, Richard Burton and Elizabeth Taylor

Second row (left to right): Eddie Fisher, Miss Louisiana

Third row (left to right): Betty Lin, Chinatown, Liza Todd, Hap Tivey

Fourth row (left to right): Rhys Tivey, Quinn Tivey